Repetition Nineteen

Mónica de la Torre

T0161722

NIGHTBOAT BOOKS
NEW YORK

ISBN: 978-1-64362-014-5

Typeset in Univers and Bembo
Graphic Design: Brian Hochberger

Cataloging-in-publication data is available from
the Library of Congress

Nightboat Books
New York
www.nightboat.org

Repetition Nineteen

CONTENTS

1

2

3

4

Replay

Isometry

Gaze trained on gaze
positioned in front of the groove
between mirror panels.
Split.
Wobbling at the edges of
both frames during tree
pose particularly.

★

A translation is moving
every point of a shape the same distance in the same direction.

★

Not ambidextrous I keep silent I understand
the dilemma of playing protagonist prefer a supporting role
the only part of your body remaining undisciplined
detached I am disobedient writes my left hand.

Unlike *nostos, algo* is unspecified.

nunca sé por dónde empezar, así que decido hacerlo al comerme
    una fresa
incontable la cantidad de semillas
can you say I'm of two minds?
yo diría que tengo ideas encontradas
lo cual abre dos posibilidades: que se encuentren como amigas
cada una con su punto de vista
hace tanto que no se ven
o que estén a punto de agarrarse
getting at each other's throats
pensé que era un mexicanismo, pero no
you're getting territorial
lo cual a ti nunca te preocupa
what are you talking about
si lo que dices es o no un regionalismo
te tiene sin cuidado, no te define
since I'm just passing through, you mean
pero te fuiste quedando
I went on staying
who's I anyway
quién habla

ay, interjección para expresar muchos y muy diversos moviemientos
del ánimo, y más ordinariamente aflicción
o dolor

ay, pronounced *I*, interjection used to express a range of mood shifts,
and more commonly affliction
or pain

★

I never know where to begin so I pick up a strawberry
with its countless seeds
¿cómo dices tengo ideas encontradas?
I am of two minds
como si en tu cerebro se alojaran dos mentes
or your skull had a Siamese twin
lo cual te haría excepcional
but it's a set phrase, the language figurative
or formulaic
its referent, a common affliction
me hiciste pensar en réferis
who plays arbiter is up for grabs
volvemos a los agarrones
don't get ahead of yourself
volvemos a las cabezas
ahead not *a head*
¿por qué no dices la verdad?
te pierdes en tus juegos de palabras
you interrupted me
up for grabs, to be for the taking,
o sea disponible, you misinterpret
to get your point across

I, pronunciado *ay*, primera persona singular en inglés

I, pronounced *ay*, first person singular

★

It follows that *algo*, an indeterminate something, from the Latin,
is unrelated to *algos*, *pain* in Greek,

de ahí se desprende que *algos*, del griego,
poco tiene que ver con *algo*, del latín.

The rest there's no need to spell out.

Discontinuous Repetition

You'd like to keep things simple, elemental.
Avoid tying yourself into knots over what you can't
come to grips with—
dark drives, miscalculations, the facts around the clock.

Or else, arrange your twined strands into arresting patterns.

Or else—
the ring of those two words roping you in.
Roped off is the alternative,
but you know it's pointless to keep things separate.

Pretend you are given enough rope.
What will you do with it next?
Rope-a-dope.

While you consider options, I salute
how quietly you defy flatness,
your multipurpose materiality.

Who's *you* by the way?
It's difficult to say.
I tangles up easily.

★

"the incidental beauty of non-objects"

*

A reluctant shaman in the guise of a nuisance—a screeching child—
promises to purge us subway riders of our general discontent. Let the
wind of change speak through his squalls and babble. Dada. Think
of it as anti-poetry produced by tiny but sturdy windpipes. He too
embraces the formless, rejects the regime.

*

Mobilized is the experience
of confusion where the familiar is made
unfamiliar, and vice versa.

A woman massaged by her partner on the subway platform,
his fists hot stones: "You're a scared animal."
Did I mishear that?

Stone in Korean 돌 is also anniversary.
Precious stones are reminders but other types of petrifaction
commemorate the past too, change it into object.
Take stones dangling from a wood beam, they
appear yielding through sheer optical effect.

On the opposite end of the spectrum
are monuments.
Puddles undo their monumentality, turn
statues and towers into shimmering surfaces on the sidewalk.

It's slippery outside. Hovering cautiously, we too
negotiate between gravity's pull
and our vertical aspirations.

A mirrored image is a non-material
photograph, an event.

The same goes for the choreography of banners waving
in the air. They announce nothing
but an otherwise invisible presence.

It's audible, though, as if chasing away something.
Earworms, for one.

What the wind has to say today it says only in passing.

Boxed In

Heads up, false friends use familiarity as camouflage.
In the source language *deciduous* might be confused with apathy,
but nothing could be further away from *desidia* than the timed
    impermanence of leaves.
Yes, even forests engage in a form of family planning.
We took for granted the tree outside our window until it failed to bud.
A gingko, they cut it down when the building across the street went up.
Since our view is limited, we like to imagine the situation from the
    missing tree's perspective.
Given the recent turn of events, it might have resisted blooming.
It was protesting its decorative use to boost property values.
Or perhaps after millennia of honing its particulars, it refused
    "the magic of tree-lined streets."
Concrete blocks these social beings' access to fungal networks,
prevents their roots from interconnecting.
Are you a reluctant loner like the specimens that surround us here today?
I hope you understand I don't mean to ruin the relationship.

Intimacy in Discourse:
A Comedy In Three Movements

After paintings by Thomas Nozkowski

One

Stick Man steps back
containing multitudes
of hues. "Ta-da!" he mouths,
since he's mostly
narrow bands
of diffused colors,
a rainbow, faded,
except for the saturated,
tender-looking red
square for a heart
and the sore ball
of his left foot
supporting the tilt.
Not to mention the display
of acid green
on the crown of his head
and wrist, signaling
the mind–body connection.
The histrionics
in the perfect tension
between dexter and sinister.
Welcome to showbiz.

Two

This binary roadblock here
demands that you back off
to keep on contemplating it.
It fancies itself a zebra
standing on diamond-patterned stilts
for camouflage's sake
and fastens itself to an equally
ornamented attachment
as if to hide from its handlers.

Forget it, it's not interested
in establishing any rapport with you.

Blame it on instinct; it knows
how coveted equids are in the North
American private sector.

Three

Here's your morality tale,
an optical conundrum/psychoactive puzzle:
the dominant lines lock,
while the areas they delimit contain
other lines within, of the faint,
disjointed variety.

Like interconnected
people and the basic story lines they each cling to
to remind themselves of themselves.
Yes, this is redundant.

In this picture, both
types of lines compete
for your attention, so that the eyes'
only resting spot
is a central area where color
has enough room to settle.

That old positing of linear
thought patterns versus the dispersal
of feelings and their counter–
tendency to ground.

In the source language *disparate*,
pronounced *dis-pah-rah-teh*, is *nonsense*.
Place an accent on the wrong
syllable and it becomes "shoot yourself."
Let's not overthink this.

Divagar

"There's a lot of waiting in the drama of experience."
Lyn Hejinian, *Oxota*

No signal from the interface except for a frozen half-bitten fruit.
Other than that, no logos. An hour is spent explaining

to the group what I've forgotten, to do with the mistranslation
of a verb that means *drifting* but can imply deviance.

The next hour goes by trying to remember, in the back of my mind,
the name of the artist who makes paintings on inkjets.

Why I'd think of him escapes me. Now my gaze circles the yoga bun
of the tall woman in front of me. I didn't pay $20 to contemplate

the back of her head. It's killing me. The pillars and plaster
saints with their tonsures floating amid electronic sound waves.

At such volume they could crumble. The virgin safe in a dimly lit
niche as the tapping on my skull and the clamor of bones or killer

bees assaults the repurposed church. This is what I sought, while
in another recess I keep hearing Violeta's "*Volver a los diecisiete*"

and seventeen-year-olds marching against the nonsense of arming
teachers. If I were an instrument. A bassoon. In the source language

we don't say "spread the word." *Pasa la voz* is our idiom, easily
mistaken for a fleeting voice. From the back row all I see is fingers

gliding in sync with her vocalizations. How fitting a last name
like halo. Lucky for us here time is measure and inexplicable

substance. That's when I decide to stop fighting the city. Use it in my
favor. Speak to strangers. Demolish the construct in the performance.

La sottise

It dawned on me, the other day, at the launch
of a former colleague's book, that if I ever
was a funny poet, I no longer was one.

I'd picked something amusing to read since
the party would be at a bar, and people wouldn't
want to stay still and listen to us drone on

but instead would be there to drink and celebrate
their friend's accomplishment, no matter what
they actually thought of his poems; they

were good poems, don't get me wrong. Alright,
they were somewhat sincere, a bit saccharine,
but that's beside the point, and, anyway, who cares.

During my reading no one chuckled loud enough
to let me know that my humor had landed.
Granted, it was subtle. My poem had to do

with the people you encounter in hotels when,
if you think about it, you're doing some of the most
intimate things you could possibly do, except

die, in the company of strangers, always
perfect. As I was saying, I was up on stage,
and couldn't see anyone. The mic was too big, right

in my face, and when I read in settings like these
all I hear is the distortion of my amplified
voice, which makes me jumble lines and garble

words I have no difficulty pronouncing otherwise.
Automobile, for example, which I can say easily
in Spanish and from now on will always be *vehicle.*

I was done and the crowd applauded, sort of.
It was the next poet's turn and everyone around me
started cheering and slapping their thighs,

and then the next poet went up, and told
hysterical jokes about Trump and Ted Cruz
as he read poems that were even wittier.

Everyone was in stitches. That's when it dawned
on me that perhaps I'm not funny anymore, but what
the hell, how's that the marker of a work's ability

to move its audience, I mean, what if Emily Dickinson
were at an open mic delivering the poem about feeling
like a nobody talking to other nobodies and everyone

cracked up, or what if it was Baudelaire,
for that matter, who had to pause up there while reading
the sonnet about nature being a temple sending people

mixed messages, because of the audience's hoots,
or better yet, imagine Catullus, reluctantly playing
to the crowd with his I love my hate and hate my love.

Why? you ask. All I know is the feeling's back
again, and it torments me. But, wait, let's circle back
to Baudelaire. What if he called out the phonies

at a gig and people misheard and exploded
with laughter, thinking he'd said *funnies* even after
he doubled down and said he wasn't kidding.

Error Is Boundless

We tried using tally marks instead, for seeming more
discrete. While adding them up one of us kept texting the other
one of us, sending photos of bright green cakes with rings
of pink icing on their edges and trios of blue flowers
adorning their tops. Single-digit price tags sticking out
from toothpicks, as if for birthdays pre-nineteen ninety nine.
Soon it got challenging to keep count while referring to each
number as a number that is one more than the previous number,
indefinitely. A lemon-yellow cake appeared onscreen and it became
evident progression would only lead back to the beginning.
One is a version of *unus*, *oinos*. In other words, listen to us.
Two mirrors *tú*, and also. When a single unit is no longer the case,
one becomes reciprocal, a second person. At the end of you
and me, three becomes expected, except when misread.
Thríe or *threo*, gender dependent. God, a prisoner or king,
laughing away. What to make of the thief in *fif*, of oil lamps
especially, as in *quinqués*, and pent up. I skipped four.
Quattuor, squatter, since four is for all when being walled off.
Time stamp: 4 pm. I meant not to demonstrate but to delve
into the full expression of the form, yet it kept emptying
out, becoming non-tiered.

Interjet 2996

"Había una vez…" is how most fairy tales begin in Spanish. It's somewhere between the English equivalents "Once upon a time…" and "There was once…." You wouldn't use it as an opener for a casual anecdote, since it instantly indicates to the reader or listener that the account to follow is fictional. Yet it does so without heightening the language as much as "upon" does in the English phrase, where a subtle literary flourish places the narrative squarely within fantasy, outside of ordinary time.

And so <u>one</u> time I was flying back to JFK from Mexico City—whose pair of synonymous names, by official decree and a mighty branding effort, had been reduced to one since I'd last spent an extended period of time there. As of January 29, 2016, the city would be referred to as Ciudad de México only. DF was no longer. On billboards, buses, and all over the streets there was signage to remind its inhabitants of the megalopolis's catchier social-media era moniker: CDMX. The city is now recognized as its own entity, and has its own governor. CDMX as an acronym might look good, but it is impossible to pronounce or swerve into vernacular. Its vowels don't snap together the way DF's do, producing the coinages *De-Efe* and its attendant *defeños* to refer to those born in the capital, such as myself. Using the acronym for its past status as a federal district made me sound like I was stuck in the past century, a friend corrected me over a text message.

Suspended now many feet away from the city's confines, <u>a</u> woman in her seventies across the aisle in the row behind mine keeps calling my name. By the second time she does this I am well aware of the fact that she isn't talking to me, but regardless, each time I hear my name, my reflex is to turn around ever so slightly. The older woman's calls are invariably met with <u>silence</u>. My namesake must have <u>a</u> low voice that can't rise above the rumble of the plane's engine, I figure. She's directly behind me, so I can't tell if she's just nodding her head or lifting her gaze. Then I hear my namesake <u>flare</u> up. One of her kids has taken <u>a sip of</u> his brother's juice and they've gotten into a fight. I spot a <u>coffee</u> stain on my jeans; I'd forgotten to clean them <u>before</u> getting on the plane. "*¡Ya párenle!* Stop <u>it</u>!" I go to the lavatory and get a glimpse of her, even though I've barely tasted the pastry the flight attendants just delivered. She'd sounded harsh, so I thought there'd be something bitter about her features. I had expected her to look somewhat like me but I am relieved to find out that we have nothing in common other than our age (past forty but otherwise indeterminate). She seems content but a bit hardened, and has the worn look of those who resent that minding other people's business is precisely their business. Before me is the image of a family with a purpose as a unit; the older woman is probably my namesake's mother or mother-in-law. They speak to each other with a distance amplified by the gap between their seats. Back in my place I notice that as audible as the older woman is, her mouth is but a tiny hole. Her two grandchildren, whom she barely speaks to, are identical twins. I know nothing of her and her family, and yet I can imagine a banker son or son-in-law waiting for them in their Tribeca or Dumbo apartment.

We are in an in-between state. When aboard a plane, there is hardly a trace of the roads we have traveled in order to get on the vessel taking us to our one shared destination, no matter how brief our stay in it may be before each of us takes our own path. And yet a counterargument can be made, as demonstrated by the exercise I've been engaging in, not deliberately. Traces of our past are etched onto our skins like tattoos, on the words we speak, like accents that resist elimination. They are there for that rare type of person with a pair of eyes and ears curious enough to be drawn away from mediating devices. Most passengers seem to be napping now. What visions parade through their minds' eyes? And how many of these visions are mirrors of sights actually seen? Are the two identical or reversed?

I imagine myself in my own bed later that night, when my experience of CDMX falls into another dimension, with its own dictates and laws—the dimension of the remembered and consequently distorted. I cannot predict how much I'll forget given what I've already forgotten. Forgetting will have to be forgiven. For getting/for giving: two sides of the same coin affording one the possibility to move on. Lights out and one self dislocates, only to appear again in the next place conjuring it.

And yet this flight joins the two of us. One resides temporarily in New York, the other left Mexico City decades ago. One has children; the other does not. One is going on, or has gone on, a family trip;

24

the other one is alone, returning from visiting family. To be sure, more than <u>three</u> contrasting equations could be made, over <u>three</u> comparisons positing us as antipodes. The could have been—<u>is</u> it a thing if it exists in the mind? Is it like <u>peace</u>, which you can sense but cannot test? <u>And/or</u>. <u>A pledge</u> to myself to leave home, back when I might not have understood the implications of doing so, had resulted in the me in this row instead of the me in the row behind. That makes me neither <u>an accomplice</u> nor <u>an enemy</u> to her, whom I overhear on <u>three</u> other instances during the flight. First telling her kids what to do, then singing along to the clapping game they play to pass the time.

Now the older woman, sensing my attentiveness to her, starts addressing me from across the aisle with a jarring familiarity. She can't <u>open</u> the switch to release her tray table. I can't tell what she wants to put on it; I don't think she has <u>books</u> or printed matter on her. I'm on this plane ride and I could be making art if I were Nina Katchadourian. Just hand me an in-flight magazine and <u>three grains</u> of rice or a packet <u>of salt</u>. I don't bring up Nina randomly. This is how I remind myself that I am supposed to be working on an interview I did with her about <u>four</u> weeks ago. My to-dos project me further into distant <u>times</u>. I might have <u>said a name</u> pertaining to her photographs taken aboard airplanes wrong: "Seating Arrangements" instead of "Seat Assignment." <u>And</u> if I did, she said <u>nothing</u> about the mistake, sparing me the embarrassment.

I doubt my namesake's noticed me. The third time I overhear her, she's telling her sons a story. They might be around <u>four</u>: "This <u>is</u> <u>the</u> story of a pair of twins, the <u>same</u> <u>as</u> you <u>two</u>! <u>If</u> they were apart, they felt like they were missing one of their hands' <u>five</u> fingers. And yet they were on their own at certain <u>times</u>. <u>You</u> might <u>ask</u> <u>yourself</u>: 'When? <u>What</u> happened when they were alone?' What I <u>am</u> saying is that much as they liked each other's company, when it came to <u>doing</u> stuff together, they didn't always see eye to eye." "What's that?" one of them says, "You mean eye to eye like from <u>here</u> to there?" He must have poked his brother in the eye, because he let out a whimper. She ignores it and continues with the story: "They didn't always agree. One of them liked to <u>burn</u> things. Small stuff, not, like, <u>your</u> <u>bed</u> or furniture or anything, but paper cups and plates, magazines, wrappers, that sort of thing." "And his parents <u>let</u> him do <u>it</u>?" asks the other twin. "No, they didn't let him <u>burn</u> things, but he'd go ahead <u>and</u> do it anyway. And when he did, the other one would <u>split</u>, because he was terribly afraid of fire. But then he'd feel heartsick from being away from his brother, and would keep coming back."

We land in New York. We each go our own way. A conversation between us might have been a letdown. I am back in the place that's been my home for as long as I lived south of the border. My other city recedes into a past whose contours keep going the way of DF.

A smoke alarm goes off. Untimely, like another alarm that a few months later, on September 19, 2017, would be set off by seismic activity near CDMX. The epicenter was so close to the city that the experiencing of the earthquake coincided with its warning. Unbelievably, there'd been a drill earlier that day, so people thought it was all a simulacrum until they realized the ground was rattling beneath their feet. Only in fiction could a deadly earthquake happen a few hours after a drill, in the same place, and on the same day, as a deadlier one thirty-two years earlier.

Equivalences

Equivalencias

One. A silence, a flare.
A sip of coffee before it tasted bitter.
A gap in a hole.

Two roads to one path
and a pair of napping eyes.
How many mirrors are two.
Night falls and two lights appear,
two children going on three.

Three is peace and a pledge,
an accomplice, an enemy.
Three open books, three grains of salt.

Four times I said a name and nothing.
Four is the same as two.

If five times you ask yourself
what am I doing here, set your bed on fire,
let it burn, and split.

Uno. Un silencio, una llamarada.
Un sorbo de café antes de que supiera amargo.
Un hoyo dentro de un agujero.

Dos caminos para una trayectoria
y sus ojos cerrados durmiendo la siesta.
Cuántos espejos son dos.
Cae la tarde y aparecen dos luces,
dos hijos que ya son tres.

Tres es paz y garantía,
un cómplice, un enemigo.
Tres libros abiertos, tres granos de sal.

Cuatro veces dije un nombre y nada.
Cuatro es lo mismo que dos.

Y si cinco veces te preguntas
qué hago aquí, quema tu cama
déjala arder, y vete.

Conversions

One. One silence, one flame.
A sip of coffee before it tasted bitter.
A prick inside a hollow.

Two roads yet one path
and eyes closed during a nap.
How many mirrors are two.
Evening falls and two moons appear,
Two offshoots that are already three.

Three is peace and the promise
of a friend and a foe,
three open books, three grains of salt.

Four times I said your name, to no avail.
Four is equal to two.

And if five times you ask yourself,
What am I doing here? set your bed on fire,
let it burn, and leave.

Equivalences

One silence, a flash.
A sip of coffee before I knew bitter.
A hole in a hole.

Two paths to a path
and his eyes closed napping.
Many mirrors are twofold.
Late afternoon and see two lights,
two sons and three.

Three is peace and security,
an accomplice or an enemy.
Three books open, three grains of salt.

Four times a name and nothing said.
Four is the same as two.

And if you ask five times
What am I doing here, burning your bed,
let it burn and go.

The Poem Is Titled Equivalencies

There's some silence, the serving of something that's bitter,
   I know that.
And there's something inside something else.

There's two roads from a source and—
wow, my memory these days!—
Oh yeah, your eyes are closed during a nap.
Yeah, mirror something, there's two somethings.
There's two lights and two boys and then there's three.

There's three open books and three grains of salt.
And there's something else I didn't understand.
And some complicit enemy.

Four times I call your name and nothing.
Four times is the same as two times.

Five times, or the fifth time, is the same.
I call your name, and… I don't hear you.
I'm sensing that the person to whom the poem is addressed
is as distracted as I am right now.
Someone isn't listening to something.

Equivalent Equivalence

A mute flare-up
a sip of coffee before the bitter one knew about it.
A hole inside a whole two roads
and a pair of sleeping eyes.
How many mirrors are there too?
The afternoon tumbles and two lights pop out
two children passing as tú.
3 space guarantee
the promise of a complex and an enemy
free open books, 3 grams of salt.
I said four asterisks and named nothing.
What is the same as _____ ?
Yes, 5 times you wonder what I do here?
Light your bed on fire, let it combust and divide itself.

Like in Valencia

The silence of Esmeralda.
The sorbet at the café is superior.
The oil at the dentist was relaxing.

The two roads were doubly tragic.
The serrano peppers caused me to take a long nap.
The quantity of spectators was twice as large.
The guy was a little slow on Sunday.
The two eels seem like three.

Three in space is guaranteed.
Whoever is complacent with me is my friend.
Three books that have beards
look grand in the sun.

Four as a number is nothing.
Four amuses two.

Five is a vessel.
Something to do with water....water is the key to five.
Camel to camel, they like to eat green.

Your Turn

`The quiet before an announcement.

A mouthful of coffee.

Then the acrimony—the acrimony!—in such bitter substitutions.

At the pass there were two roads.

I closed my eyes and speculated if they were mirrored.

Not to say that I took this to be true on the basis of insufficient evidence, like in the tome.

My reflection lacked such polish.

One thing was clear: all three of them had parents.

Peace, security, sure. But also accomplices, enemies.

Call them what you will.

Collaborators, cronies, reciprocal minions, nursing their resentment.

A symbol, a distinctive designation, an epithet, even a record.

When anything could be a name, two people might as well be four.

What to do here?

I'm no baker.

I could make you a place in which to lie.

Please let me burn.

Picture Character

Finger pointing up. Zipper–Mouth Face,
and an angular burst of orange and red in star-like shape.
Scrunched Eyes after a hot beverage.
A heavy large red circle that stands for what is correct in Japan.
There is room inside of rightness for what is right.

A Pedestrian faces two motorways.
Eyeballs shut turn into Sleeping Face.
A selfie of a selfie leads to question mark.
Night sky, two light bulbs.
Family: Man, Woman, Girl, Boy, followed by number three.

Dove, ring,
Grinning Face with Smiling Eyes. Pouting Face is snubbed.
Three books plus saltshaker.

Four clocks show different random times.
Speaking Head emits registered sign, then empty speech balloon.
Four equal sign two.

Five clocks show different random times.
Thinking Face, index pointing to a world map, question mark.
Flames plus bed, plus flames and more flames
and person running with large stride and arms outstretched.

If has no pictogram.

Same As It Ever Was

One. A pregnant pause. A flash in the pan.
One sip of whiskey, then the burn in your throat.
A redacted redaction.

Two options, one fate,
someone dozes in the middle of the day.
Where's the source utterance in an echo chamber.
Nightfall lights lights,
grapes come in clusters.

Three is surety and truce,
the perceived threat before an alliance.
Three open windows, three specks of dust.

I call four times and no one answers.
Four times or two, whatever.

If you're tossing and turning all night
going, Where am I? over and over and over
and over and over, it's time to burn your bridges
and move on.

Self-Mastery

We thank you for your interest, an urge from within, a special something.
A sea of metaphysical books before they amounted to clairvoyance.
An ether inside a higher ether.

Two sensitivities to one whole
and a dimension of your dormant psychic abilities.
How many invisible helpers are mirrors.
Ancient truths test and two subscribing religious backgrounds,
two teachings that fall beyond the Desire World.

Three is to awaken through solar currents;
a dense body, a tool and a hindrance.
Three activities, three additional mediums.

Four times the association benefits unused sex force.
Four taps into the same harmonious personal relationships.

If five innovative solutions connect in the cerebrospinal nervous system,
periodically conjure the acme of materiality, play the aura,
organize preceding exercises, and travel to a temple.

Equanimity

One ball, one pitch, one one players,
or one one after another, meaning eleven.
Hands off. One red card, one player down,
meaning ten, or zero after one.
Here an odd color theory applies:
a red made of two yellows.
Two teams, two goals. The mass
of spectators both present and viewing
remotely may or may not avoid such clear-
cut binaries while following
trinities: two teams running after a ball
so live it could be animate.
This leads to the occasional
tangle of legs.
The possible configurations of one one players
as a unit in the course of ninety minutes tends to
infinity, yet on average, per game, goals fall
between two and three.
In the end, all tournaments come down to four
teams vying for two slots, and an eventual return
to square one, since draws are ruled out.
Shootouts are the corrective. Skill succumbs
to guesswork, a stand-in for fate, to be met one-on-one,
per usual. If five penalty kicks don't untie the score,
add another five. Then wonder whether
ardor leads to pain in equal amounts.

Numbers As Qualifiers

Ablaze.

Twofold mirrors
seeing in and out during sleep.

A, B, and C.
And consequent deals between parties.
Sooner than you know, three becomes etcetera.

A way of living,
or the route that a computer operating system follows
through directories on a disk to locate a file.
A noun four times and nothing done.

What are you doing burning through layers,
ask five times
and eagerly. Then flee.
Just go. Zeros and ones.
Here.

Equivalence

January 1 flare
silently sipped coffee
before a super bitter self
into a hole.

Two paths as a path
and his eyes closed
napping as many mirrors.
Evening falls and two lights appear
and are 3
Don Quixote.

Press space
guarantee an accomplice
an enemy
three books
open.

4 months
a man says nothing
4 is the same
as two.

5 times and if you wonder
why I'm here
burning gel
drum great
song and old age.

Llamaradas Are Blow Jobs

Two paths to a
network and
pulse hates
hot chicken
fingers.
And endemic dressings.

Resist cantata. An enemy
Safe 3rd 3-pro
equipment when stresados.

And four thirds
of Control
investigates
whether a
name and the
same two.

Two ways to pay a criminal
For her and her
son draws two
men in the
party, Thor.

August 3rd
floors are all
going to hear
last two digits
showers.

8 say yes.

4 same gestures.

5 of us
resist questions
and another will fuck chuck.

Equivocation

UNO. Um solemnly, Ina llama dada.
Um Sorbonne de café antes de que super smart.
Um boho denture de um sfumato.

Dos casinos para ulna trajectories
Y sue know surmise do la siesta.
Chanting selenide son dos
Car la yard y spared dos lives,
Dos yoyos queen ya son tres.

Tres Esc. pass y Varangian,
Um compile, um evenly.
Tres libidos abort, tres franks de sal.

CIA vexes duh dime too bomb y nada.
CIA Esc. lo gizmo queer dos.

Y Si cinch vexes etc. pregnant
Queen aqua queer too came
Female ardor y veteran.

Birdwatching

puerta corrediza
Behind the sliding glass door, a cinderblock wall
bloque de ceniza

demarcates a small concrete patio.
tangible

A window-shaped opening frames a shrub
oportunidad

of many branches growing on the slope.
sucursales

Or is intended to frame, if intentionality can be attributed to a hole.
incriminar

The shrub, like all living things, surpasses the wall's edges.
barreras

Two dirt-covered outdoor chairs, of a hue
autoridades   sombra

of blue that wavers between deep sky blue and azure.
triste   ondear en medio de

Facing each other and empty, their colors mirror
                    vano   su carácter
the plastic in the abandoned dustpan and broom at the outer edge,
                    perdido

tilting toward the soil, as if to sweep it up.
                              redada

The cleaning liquid's solvents discolored the chairs
                                        autoridades

Three chemical agents account for the faded hue:
                                  desvanecido

denatured alcohol, methyl alcohol, and ethyl acetate.

                    estrechos
Four continuous, discrete sounds, all announcing nothing:
a screech, a hammering, a siren, a buzz.
                    nereida   cuchicheo, telefonazo

hacer chatarra   de nervios
Totaling five. The top edges of the patio's walls and an angular adja-
cent roof jut against the landscape to bring geometry into sharper
focus. The building knows what to do there.   penetrante

45

Updated Prior Inscription

Behind a gliding glass door, a wall made of blocks of ash
demarcates a small tangible patio.
A window-shaped opportunity frames a shrub
with many subsidiaries growing on the slope.
Or intends to incriminate, if we can attribute intentionality to a hole.
The shrub, like all living things, surpasses the border's edges.

A couple of grimy authorities outside, of a shadow
of sadness suspended amid deep sky blue and azure.
Before one another and hollow, their character mirrors
the plastic in a dissolute dustpan and broom at the outer edge,
tilting toward the dirt, as if to raid it.

The debt-free agents distress the authorities.
Three ghosts behind the vanished hue:
non-naturalized, methane-derived, once associated with ether.

Four continuous, finite channels, all announcing nothing:
a screech, a hammering, a mermaid, a ring.

Wrecking five. The superior nerves of the patio's walls and an angu-
lar adjacent roof jut against the landscape to bring geometry into an
invasive focus. The structure knows what to do there.

A Big, Beautiful Wall

One. No din, a flash.
A sip of a hot drink made from roasted and ground seeds found bitter
    after swallowing.
A bottomless pit.

Twofold roads, one path
and shut eyes, unawake.
Two looking glasses are how many?
With dusk come lights.
Two children, now three.

Three is oath, is stillness,
a chum, a foe.
Three truths, three lies.

Four times the speaker said nothing.
Four and two are the same.

Having asked five times
why she'd stay there, she set the bed on fire
and left, letting it burn.

La más mimética de todas

one resists breaking, stoical,
a form of integrity to a
silence it's sensible to keep, concerning
a perfunctory this or that, a
flicker which is not the North American woodpecker, but
a flash alert coursing through your system like a
sip of a beverage you'd confused with something else, say,
of wine when you were expecting
coffee, which must also stimulate
before being acknowledged as having provided
it, *it* standing for excitability, circularly, still I
tasted the syrupy liquid and instead of
bitter I found it cloying, a tad tangy.
a donut
hole, say, one covered by a hibiscus glaze, wouldn't taste thus.
in no time does
a query about its nature lead to the thought that a
hole is not always an absence. from a donut derive
two holes, the edible one, of which samples are said to be "dunked" on
roads across the nation, meaning, at the rest stops providing respite
    from them,
to be clear, and the missing
one whose removal has left a mark in the donut itself. its
path, like that of loss
and that of lack, is
a riddle, or an enigma.
pair this with the trash collection taking place on the level
of cells while we're
napping, or with the way our

eyes do not mirror whatever it is that our souls might not be.
how is not only how but also how
many ways do we not know ourselves.
mirrors, in their inscrutability, prompt these questions, and they
are never answered by anyone except for the
two girls who last
night retold the parable of the tree that
falls in Silicon Valley
and there is no one there to hear it except for
two girls who like to turn everything into a parable. they spoke of
lights or luminous orbs that
appear anytime the
two of them talk about the
kids who once were not so merrily
going on a hike
on the grounds of a historic villa.
three kids, it was
three of them, plus a schoolmate/guardian who
is not much older than they are then. the times were not of
peace, but it wasn't wartime either,
and a sense of menace lurked everywhere around. they had made
a promise to each other, a
pledge to not leave the trails until
an antagonistic force compelled them to. the guardian was no
accomplice, he had not even
an inkling of the kids' plans to turn him, maybe, into an unwilling
enemy. nobody did either. these
three kids had chosen to
open themselves to the types of adventures they'd read about in
books. none of the
three suspected who would be adversary. they had
grains in their backpacks (instant oats) and some pieces

of fruit. also nuts without
salt, lest they get thirsty. the
four of them were seen more than a few
times by other hikers, they later testified.
I might have even seen them,
said one of the girls. once
a few days had passed the
name of the guardian was all over the news.
and so were the kids', but those meant
nothing, since they were aliens, said the other girl. the
four of them vanished never to be seen again. that
is not the story's punch line, however.
the point of the parable is never the
same. one telling is told
as if to scare people, conspiring, the
two girls, to spook their audience, as
if they were in the haunted villa about to wrap their
five fingers around an unsuspecting listener's neck. other
times they're aiming to gaslight
you. they involve you in their mind games so you
ask why they'd be telling the story to someone such as
yourself, who's just passing through.
what can be gleaned, I
am certain of it, is this: if
I were to ask about what hearing the parable is
doing to you, I might get stuck
here, one of the girls said. her hair was down and starting to
burn; this is not
your ordinary vision. I'm not even in
bed yet but I
let my eyes close till
it is time to open them again, who knows when. a

burn in the other girl's chest shines through my closed lids,
and it is almost ghastly, but not quite. a
split second later I hear the tree fall.

Mother to Daughter

You feel that dose of adrenaline gushing through your body before
you open your mouth to say it's not enough, no, it's not enough to
say something's not enough either, just like it's not enough to step
back to take a picture of a view that almost leaves you breathless,
no, the camera will never see what you see and insufficiency keeps
invading forests as much as eucalyptus trees, was what she said before
she threw what remained in her cup into the sink, for bitterness has
never been her thing, and she added that, apropos of insufficiency, it
is not comparable to the sum of negative and positive numbers which
sometimes, only sometimes, end up cancelling a sign as if by magic.

There was a fixed destiny, but the routes toward it were many
and just contemplating them made her lethargic. Upon opening her
eyes she looked in the mirror and saw her pupils reflecting the image
of herself looking in the mirror. It was nighttime, and had she not
turned on the light, her triplicated image would not have appeared to
her with the definition of aluminum on a plate of glass.

The enemy becomes infiltrated to the point of becoming indistin-
guishable from the friend. Upon their fusion both achieve the same
degree of cruelty. Likewise the scattered grains of salt, boding bad
luck in plain sight, but for whom, is the question no one asks.

I nonetheless didn't say it in vain, since by saying "the less" I
conjured insufficiency again, and if we're talking about repetition's
consequences, that there have been some, it has been proven.

In hindsight, deep into your flight's course, your words shone
lighter, in all the splendor of their opacity.

Equivocal Valences

A noun, a silent one, despite the assertiveness of such parts
of speech. An IOU of sorts, from a person like a lama, not a llama,
ridding us of free radicals, figuratively, with his glowing orbs.
I nursed a decaf while he upped the ante, promising pie in the sky.
A woman named Margo explained that although holmium (Ho) plays
no biological role in humans, its salts quicken your metabolism.

"There's a dent in my car! It's no hot rod, but still," some guy nagged
as I was heading back on my bike. I'd either done damage or it was a scam.
I preferred not to spar, so produced an ashtray, since he was fuming.
He went on hectoring. I, a bit deferential for the sake of all of us,
and that of my radius, kept my unruffled mien (à la Alcott) and got away
                                        singing do re mi fa sol la siesta...

In the dream, there is an infant son, and I am elated, ardently motherly
despite the kids' yapping. Are they ever to end? Osmium (Os) is the densest
of natural elements, Margo says, now in the dream. Lucky for me,
I get a dose of instruction while I yak about my son. In medias res,
I can be such as spaz, I've forgotten the man's rant. I've got a companion
and have missed that my kid's got lice and might need an enema. I go on

ad-libbing and ask Rosa, who also happens to be Margo, if she too is bifid,
snake-like. Osmium is the densest of natural elements. She utters
repeated nos; our differences become salient. "Where's the trove of
    documents I found?

Their relevance might be nominal, but still." She brays, laughing, "Nada;
no sé nada. At least it's not roe," almost in slo-mo.

This is unrealism. Its dos and don'ts made corporeal. Take a step, face a gun. No one's haggling. With her IQ, I'd rise from the mat, steady my cam, record déjà vu, and arduously vet elements such as these.

Hola, Mi Amor

1.

u enter an abode, a silo, or an asylum
u signal to a code man
u a u
u fun
u genderqueer
indeed
an uproar
achoo
soju

2.

eyes as door
supine u see da moon's outline soar across a luminous circle
jet crescent to sun's radiant rays
a ray trade
soaps dos ojos opacados
day's coda heaps

3.

similar zone disparate elements
bogus cognates
I go rest
untrap sonar
liberate cry zones

4.

dolus
I ate carb, my mom's trove o' quince, nada crudo
o my lost jeunesse

5.

language as   quimera
                cyst
                camera, hid
                tape
                cost
                queue
                evidence

¡ajay!

trouvé

Latin Lover

habitas cofre falso

el silencio
fue tu urna

beata detenta fe
fea, la temen

te propina
sendos golpes
por perderte

ay, hostia
tanto palpitar

tango fatal

tanta ironía

sale el bípedo atarantado

      en una kermés, grifo, gané y perdí peces
      encontré más "fishes"

      el shaman gritó: ¡fúmeselos, brinde!

canto doy
wagneriano
casi desentonado

huí, por no creer
fui higo y organismo

de mi mortis es tiempo ya

itinero
plié

fin

Latin Lover

a fake chest is your dwelling

silence
was your urn

holier-than-thou, she feigns faith
she's foul, and feared

she lands quite a few
blows on you
for losing yourself

holy cow!
all this palpitating

fatal tango

all this irony

exit the biped in a daze

      at a fair, stoned, I won and lost "pescados"
      I found more fishes

      the shaman screamed: smoke 'em away, to your health!

I sing
Wagnerian
almost out of tune

I split, for doubting
I was fig, and organism

of my mortis it is now the time

I itinerate
plié

the end

I was having a flashback.

Silence, scent, omission, wholeness.

One cup of coffee, one abyss, or one blackness in an abyss.

There is some chasm and there is only one abyss.

One burrow. The word *hole*.

Cup, burrow, abyss, then trace in the mirror.

A hole on hiatus.

Pit in a pit, a hole in a hole.

Hole in the gap.

Or the other way around, a gap in the whole.

A "hole in a hole" creates deficiency, it's a play on words.

By the way, what is the difference between the two?

A hole is just a hole. Either a black hole or a burrow in the ground.

A gap is a precipice and its meaning can be figurative.

Abyss in abyss?

Perhaps we can translate one of these abysses as a verb.

To disappear into an abyss.

пропасть в пропасть (*propast' v propast'*).

A sip of coffee before the feeling of bitterness.

If I understand correctly, silence and coffee were before the sense of
    bitterness.

They ruined the poem! You know, like Derrida says, translation is ruin.

That's what I do in my translation.

A hole is number one. As if the blackness were an all-encompassing unit.

About the blackness, is there a color component?

A gap is a property of a hole.

"Hiatus in abyss" is too metaphorical.

"Abyss on hiatus." Tyutchev.

One of these words can be switched for something more human.

A collapse in a hole.

Two children in the mirror become enemies, now there are three of them.

Two kids or three?

Two children come out into three.

Two roads. Two children become three... Don't remember how that happened.

I wrote down that there was one path and inside it were three roads.

Or maybe one path with three branches.

I don't remember this line very well.

I don't remember either. I just saw it as three possible ways to walk one path.

Three roads in one path.

Were there any other objects besides roads?

At night two fires light up.

It might have not happened. These memories might not have been.

Phantom retelling.

Okay, when the night comes, fires light up.

Two fires.

And what was after the fire?

Children. There were two children.

One of them is either an enemy or an accomplice.

They become enemies.

How?

Through the mirror.

I've written "Two children exit into three."

What about "they exit and see"?

I will write two variations with see and exit.

Two children see, the third one exits.

How do you say *accomplice* in Russian? I think it's very important, connected to children.

I am not a huge fan of the word *accomplice*.

They are multiplying. From two, three.

Two children become three.

From two the third is visible.

There was a mirror. Two mirrors?

How many mirrors compose two mirrors?

The mirror is a medium that provides an opportunity for multiples.

There was just a mirror and its reflection, like a number, duality.

Why don't we like "Two children see three children in the mirror?"

Two children are walking and seeing. Simply, the natural way.

When we take out the verbs, we are waiving some kind of…

In the poem itself we had more narration but for some reason we can't
    recreate it.

So we have two mirrors, two roads, three roads in one path, two fires
    lit at night, and two children. Are we going to add some action here?

If we don't remember, let's leave it alone.

Let's do this: "Two children are walking on a street."

Why "on a street"?

There was a street.

And what is the next action?

The third one comes out.

Two children are walking on the street. They see the third one come out.

This is a very Russian version. Like detective fiction.

So we have three children seeing a real third person. But when I was
listening to the poem I thought they saw *themselves* as three people.

They just triple.

Two children are walking and tripling? The word *triple* in Russian is
    bad in this case.

They triple and get upset.

троятся, расстраиваются (*troyatsya, rasstraivayutsya*).

Three people, some kind of villain.

Three open books, three specks of salt.

Next event. Let's keep going forward.

Four is the same as two. What do you think?

Four is also two.

Four is two.

Also, there was four of something, either four mares or four nightmares?

I'd like to have both because in English they're almost the same.

There is doubt. Uncertainty.

Most likely we have nightmares since there is a bed further in the poem.

Let's write "four mares slash nightmares."

Next we have riders.

We're forcing the rider and maybe he doesn't exist.

And what's up with the bed?

They burned their bed four times. Burn and cut.

Five times you ask yourself, What am I doing here? Set your bed on fire,
    let it burn and fall apart.

Break up!

Leave the building!

Everyone remembers the fifth one.

Everyone remembers a little different.

Five times question: What am I doing here?

If you ask five times.

And then the bed?

Burn the bed four times.

Oh, like the proverb.

Burn the bed four times. Does it really say "burn"?

Yeah, set it on fire.

Set the bed on fire four times. It's calmer that way.

Depends on your temperament.

Of course people have different likes.

I think I heard an imperative.

This is a gendered moment.

We can use an infinitive as middle ground. So "to light on fire" four times?

No. "Let it burn."

Is this the finale?

Then split. Let it fall apart.

Let it become ashes? It can't fall apart after a bonfire.

I think *split* is not used in the sense of "walk away from each other" about two people.

In American English *split* might mean "to leave, to flee."

Oh, so it's not about two people?

Not "to smash to pieces" but "to leave."

I nod as if I understand.

Is it happening with her?

Not "her."

I mean the author. Someone is leaving.

Now we are just deciding whether the separation happens with the bed or these strange people.

They come together and separate. There are two or three of them.

Maybe it will be more interesting even if it's a deviation of the original.

After all, we are working from memory.

So "walk away" relates not only to this action but to the whole thing.

The equivalence. The concordance.

If you ask yourself five times, What am I doing here? Set your bed on fire four times, let it burn.

Completed action or incomplete action? сгорает or пусть горит (*sgorayet* or *pust' gorit*)?

We are walking away from each other.

I'm back with divergence not because the title of the poem is also a noun but because some kind of process is taking place.

And at some stage the differences turn everything into ashes.

There is an end to the differences.

All turns into nothing.

Equivalencias

Uno. Un silencio, una llamarada.
Un sorbo de café antes de que supiera amargo.
Un hoyo dentro de un agujero.

Dos caminos para una trayectoria
y sus ojos cerrados durmiendo la siesta.
Cuántos espejos son dos.
Cae la tarde y aparecen dos luces,
dos hijos que ya son tres.

Tres es paz y garantía,
un cómplice, un enemigo.
Tres libros abiertos, tres granos de sal.

Cuatro veces dije un nombre y nada.
Cuatro es lo mismo que dos.

Y si cinco veces te preguntas
qué hago aquí, quema tu cama
déjala arder y vete.

Translation Key

T1:   Embedded translation.

T2:   Superimposed original and
        translation.

T3:   Self-translation informed by journal
        entries from 1996, the original poem's
        year of composition.

T4:   Early Google Translate version from
        2012.

T5:   Version of the poem produced by
        a person with partial knowledge of
        Spanish upon hearing the original.
        Courtesy of Jane Fine.

T6:   Composite of Google Translate
        app versions back and forth from
        Spanish and English using voice-
        recognition function, 2018.

T7:   Homophonic version produced
        on the spot by a person with
        scant knowledge of Spanish.
        Courtesy of Bruce Pearson.

T8:   Transcription of a translation into
        emojis.

T9:   Google Translate version from
        Spanish to Japanese to English,
        2018, with occasional contributions
        from Merriam-Webster.

T10:   Translation into as many idiomatic
        expressions as the original poem
        allowed.

T11:   Translation into language from a
        Rosicrucian pamphlet.

T12:   Adaptation to the language of soccer.

T13:   Associative departure.

T14:   Version produced by Google
        Translate app upon processing a
        Spanish speaker's oral delivery of
        the original.

T15:   Unedited version produced by
        the Google Translate app upon a
        non-Spanish speaker's oral delivery
        of the original. Courtesy of Bruce
        Pearson.

T16:   Unedited version produced by the
        iPhone's autocorrect function upon
        trying to text the poem via SMS.

T17: Rewriting of the poem in a different context. Only visible objects in the room in which the translation was performed could be written about in the poem.

T18: Deliberate mistranslation of poly-semic terms in T17.

T19: Version of the poem including only words with Anglo-Saxon roots.

T20: Translation of the poem smuggled inside another poem as an acrostic.

T21: Interpolation of the original.

T22: Poem written around the results of seeing the original as an ambiguous figure.

T23: Anagrammatic translation permu-tating all of the letters in the origi-nal Spanish into English-language words.

T24: Anagrammatic translation permu-tating all of the letters in an English version of the original into Spanish-language words, and its correspond-ing translation into English.

T25:   Culled from a transcript of a con-
        versation held by participants in
        an English-to-Russian translation
        workshop moderated by Matvei
        Yankelevich at The Flying Inn
        in Moscow on March 22, 2018.
        During the conversation, partici-
        pants Georgii Martirosian, Sergey
        Sdobnov, Lena Vaneyan, and
        Ekaterina Zakharkiv were in the pro-
        cess of collating their translations of
        the original from memory in order
        to produce a collective Russian ver-
        sion of the poem. The conversation
        was transcribed and translated into
        English by Elena Mironciuc.

T1:   On "Interjet 2996"

It's peach season again. I happen to be wearing a white t-shirt. I also happen to be eating a peach. At some point the juice slides down my fingers onto my white t-shirt. This happens repeatedly. All beachy, since I'm not one for spic-and-span. She once was a spic in the eyes of the paterfamilias. I shout it out if the shout's available to me. He might have been teasing. *Fastidious* is another false friend. Fussy here; there, a drag. Shouting sometimes sets the stain. Hence the camouflage.

She was me and I was her during the summers spent here, visiting from Mexico City, when she imagined that the sustained performance in which she played an American teenager was convincing to the kids on the block with whom she hung out and bonded, even. Concealment achieved not through erasure but through cluttering the surface where the thing appears amid elements competing for attention. But right under the slang she feigned being fluent in, there was another vernacular that would slacken her tongue, leading to the embarrassment of saying the right thing wrongly or the wrong thing flat-out. She said this happened to me, and became me.

Once I asked what made a poem a poem. No one replied. I only remember the episode because someone else remembered it for me.

Esta lengua dislocada, *bella nadadora, desviada para siempre de su rol acuático y puramente acariciador.* (*Altazor*) If the tongue were a beautiful swimmer. Fuzzy peach.

T2:   On "Equivalencias Equivalences"

Poetry often manifests radical departures from normative syntax, lexicon, and utterance such that its interpretation, an integral part of the translation process, involves surmising authorial intentions, the thinking goes. Translation frequently entails engaging conjecture since, in order to make decisions, translators speculate about what authors' criteria might have been for giving words specific sonic and visual arrangements; for juxtaposing images or statements, jump-cuts, and leaping from one to another without articulating the logic behind the associations propelling the poem; and for choosing to leave a lot unsaid.

Yet no matter how inventive a text may be, its language, with its corresponding rules and conventions, is a given, an adaptable ready-made whose functioning depends precisely on that very condition. One of translation's main difficulties consists in distinguishing those elements inherent in the language of the original from those that its author has created with it. In discussing various translations of Homer, Borges writes of that "difficult category of knowing what pertains to the poet and what pertains to the language. To that fortunate difficulty we owe the possibility of so many versions...."[1]

A line in "Equivalencias," a poem in Spanish I wrote in the nineties that gave rise to the slew of different translations presented here, illustrates this point. A common Spanish equivalent to the word *nightfall* is the phrase "*cae la tarde*" (literally, the afternoon falls). It is ambiguous as to whether what "falls" is the afternoon or evening, since *la tarde* refers to any time lapse between noon and dusk. One thing is certain, though: unlike in English, it is not night. And is it not night that descends upon daylight at sundown? A translator unfamiliar with such idiom might unknowingly translate it to "the afternoon falls," imparting the line with a creative and rather absurd flourish missing in the original.

Except for works in which didactic or political urgency instantly communicates their instrumental logic, the poem's intention is rarely part of its fabric. It remains outside of the text, unlike in much fiction, in which the narrator's motives for telling a story, no matter how opaque or obscure, tend to be woven into the narration itself,

1. Jorge Luis Borges, *Selected Non-Fictions,* ed. by Eliot Weinberger (New York: Penguin, 1999), 70.

becoming one of its essential components. In the realm of poetry, however, inference appears especially necessary when a poem being translated dispenses with narrative elements and displays, primarily, a performative voice—one speaking to a receiver who has to infer everything about the work exclusively from the specificities of the subject's utterances. Intention, in fact, might be the one thing that remains most opaque in a poem, even to the poet who's penned it.

The Mexican conceptual poet and artist Ulises Carrión wrote that "Just as the ultimate meaning of words is indefinable, so the author's intention is unfathomable" in the 1975 manifesto "The New Art of Making Books."[2] Forty-something years later, the statement may seem old hat, yet even the most nuanced of translators persist in invoking authorial intention as the ultimate justification for their decisions, as if writing itself were dictated by it and readers played no role in completing a work. Wittgenstein points to intention's appeal when arguing that, as a construct, it provides "the final interpretation... the thing that cannot be further interpreted"[3] and is therefore exempt from critical analysis.

When it comes to translation the issue at hand cannot be to access the poem or poet's intentions—an impossibility–but to dissect a given work's elements and then choose which to prioritize in accordance with one's own interpretation of the way in which these elements interrelate. Haroldo de Campos suggests as much in the essay "Translation as Creation and Criticism" when writing about translations as transcreations: "It is *as if* one took apart and, at the same time, put back together again the machine of creation, that frail and apparently inaccessible beauty that offers us a finished product in a foreign language but which, nevertheless, is able to give itself over to an implacable vivisection...".[4] I italicized "as if" because a literary work is not an organism whose elements can be taken apart and vivisected. Its parts are inextricable; once dissected, they morph into another text. Identifying them necessarily involves a thought experiment, an act of the imagination, and thus is an inevitably provisional activity, no

2. Guy Schraenen , ed., *Ulises Carrión: We have won! Haven't we?* (Amsterdam: Idea Books, 1992), 57.
3. Anthony Kenny, ed., *The Wittgenstein Reader* (Cambridge and Oxford: Blackwell Publishers, 1994), 75.
4. Haroldo de Campos, "Translation as Creation and Criticism", *Novas*, tr. and ed. by António Sergio Bessa and Odile Cisneros (Evanston, IL: Northwestern, 2006), 323.

matter how persuasive. Therein the foibles, and ultimately also the riches, of translation lie.

Regardless, one might think that only in the case of self-translation the problem of inferring what the author's intentions could have been when writing a poem would be null, and that choosing which elements not to sacrifice is easier. Even if intent did not overtly dictate the writing, one might imagine that the same subconscious associations that triggered composition originally may also guide the translation process, the poet–translator tapping into them when recasting the work into another language. Yet a perplexing challenge arises if those initial associations were the result of wordplay, for wouldn't the poet–translator have to suppress new ones triggered by the words in the target language, lest they pull the poem in a direction entirely different from that of the original?

In other words: How to tell apart what is signal and what is noise when the resonances of both languages are equally loud?

Rui Chafes, *The world becomes silent*, 2004, Jardim da Sereia, Coimbra (Portugal).

T3:   On "Conversions"

Let us imagine that only in the case of self-translation can intention be accessed easily. In this case, to attain the most loyal possible English version of the poem "*Equivalencias*," I could try to recall the general emotional state I was in after leaving Mexico City, while I was in the process of becoming adjusted to using English as opposed to Spanish as my primary language. To do so I could mine the journals of those early years in New York, in which I wrote most of the work that came to constitute my first book in Spanish, *Acúfenos* (2006). The title itself poses a considerable translation challenge. The Spanish Royal Academy offers the following definition of the word *acúfeno*: "auditory sensation that does not correspond to any real exterior sound." Compare it with the definition of its English equivalent, *tinnitus*, in the OED: "sensation of ringing or buzzing in the ears." Rather than denote a pathology, by titling my book *Acúfenos* I meant to address the peculiar status of poetic language, which unless experienced read or performed out loud, readers and writers alike might hear in their heads as if it were coming from an exterior. Perhaps the title also subliminally related to the status of Spanish and English at this particular moment for me—the sounds of one or the other becoming ghostly *acúfenos* when not in use.

A mnemonic exercise with the aid of a journal from 1996 seemed worthwhile to test common assumptions regarding the role of authorial intention in writing and translating. "Conversions" is a translation based on the draft of the poem written in an undated journal entry sometime between February 25 and March 7, 1996. What follows is the annotated version.

Conversions[i]

One. One silence, one flame.[ii]
A sip of coffee before it tasted bitter.
A prick inside a hollow.[iii]

Two roads yet one path
and eyes closed during a nap.[iv]
How many mirrors are two.
Evening falls and two moons appear,[v]

Two offshoots which are already three.[vi]

....

i. The poem was initially untitled. The journal is brimming with fragments and drafts of failed poems; the pervading sentiment of most entries is one of obsession with becoming a poet and forging an amorous bond with a male partner. Yet here the main preoccupation concerns the possibility of converting the matter of everyday life into poetry. Given that this transformation process bears a similarity with numerological abstraction, it seems that "Conversions" is a more fitting title for the poem than the original "Equivalences."

ii. A felicitous translation of *llamarada*, which literally means "sudden blaze." *Flame*, however, might refer also to a lover or a surge of emotion, which seems closer to the intent of the original.

iii. As much as this line could be read as a rather inept metonymical allusion to the male and female sex organs during copulation, in the original it actually refers to a doubled or magnified feeling of emptiness, which the repetition of orifices in the original is intended to heighten (both *hoyo* and *agujero* refer to holes, hollows, or orifices). The language of the original could then be read as a double view of a cavity focusing on its exterior, visible manifestation—a hole— and also on its invisible interior, a hollow. However, the double meaning of the word *prick* in English perfectly conveys the play that the original can merely suggest. Also worth noting is that in Spanish there is no distinction between *un* used as pronoun and *un* the adjectival form of *one* denoting a single unit. The numerical equivalences in the poem would require that *un* be translated as *one* throughout the stanza, but the result would be too awkward in English.

iv. There is no way of knowing who the napping subject is. This could be alluding to a post-coital scenario, or, just as easily, to the lonesome subject uttering the poem. Incidentally, I juggled multiple part-time jobs at the time and remember napping whenever possible.

v. The sense of the line is easier to grasp if the ambiguity in the literal translation "Evening falls and two lights appear" is eliminated. The draft had the moon appearing twice, not lights. The logic of the line's revision escapes me now. Two moons in an urban setting refer, naturally, to a street lamp as well as the moon, and hence exacerbate the nocturnal mood of the poem.

vi. Curiously, the draft of the poem had *higos* (figs) instead of *hijos* (children) in the line "*Dos higos que ya son tres.*" Was the poem transcribed erroneously or was that key letter changed intentionally? The word *offshoots* in English seems better than *hijos* since it retains the notion of proliferation, but applies equally to people, animals, plants, and even things.

Three is peace and the promise
of a friend and a foe,
three open books, three grains of salt.[vii]

Four times I said your name, to no avail.[viii]
Four is equal to two.[ix]

And if five times you ask yourself,
What am I doing here? set your bed on fire,
let it burn, and leave.

---

vii. The possible narrative of the poem becomes manifest by the third stanza. Again, felicitously, translation made explicit the line's undertone, the rationale for juxtaposing the "open book" phrase and an oblique reference to the other English-language idiom: "to take with a grain of salt." Three people in a relationship might think it is possible to conceal nothing from each other, but the dynamic between them is bound to shift continually given the threat of two persons establishing allegiances while leaving a third one out. The irony is that neither idiom exists in Spanish. The two were used subconsciously (and literally) in Spanish, although in that language they are not immediately understandable and might have seemed, therefore, more "poetic."

viii. The journal entry proves that the original addressed a particular *you*. When the poem in the journal was transcribed and revised, ambiguity was preferred, and therefore the line became: "Four times I said *a* name and nothing." A *nombre* in Spanish can be any noun as well as a name. The present translation is intended to avoid confusion—the line could be incorrectly read as if what was said was the phrase "a name and nothing" instead of an unspecified name. The futility of the subject's attempt to beckon the loved one—ultimately the subject is only talking to herself—leads to the severity and shift in the final stanza, where she speaks to herself in the second person, as if she were another.

ix. Again, rendering the poem in English might have improved this line, given that "to two" is a homophone of "two two," proving that four is equal to two two's.

80

T4:   On "Equivalences"

Close reading reveals that there was nothing out of the ordinary about the speaker's concerns. If they translate, it's precisely because they're rather common, and who's to find fault with that?

Apropos of commonplaces: Who doesn't consult their device when unsure of how to move forward? Enter Google Translate, the most neutral of readers, perhaps the best possible one since it has no preconceived knowledge of what it translates or of the context of an utterance, and in producing literal translations makes not only, as Borges would put it, "for uncouthness and oddity, but also for strangeness and beauty."[5] It avoids reading *into* a text and does not differentiate between, say, a poem, a legal document, or spam. It takes words at face value, since as David Bellos explains, "it doesn't deal with meaning at all. Instead of taking a linguistic expression that requires decoding, Google Translate (GT) takes it as something that has probably been said before. It uses vast computing power to scour the Internet in the blink of an eye looking for an expression in some text that exists alongside its paired translation."[6]

Although GT's methods continue to be perfected—and improved translations will surely be part of the corpus it combs through in a matter of seconds by the time you read this these observations—we can glean some of its biases from its translation of "*Equivalencias*."

For starters, GT's most egregious bias, applying to any translation of poetry, is that it expects everything not only to have been said before, but to be locatable on the internet, therefore making it ill-suited to render inventive, novel poetic utterances into another language.

Predictably, when GT is presented with multiple options, it cannot infer which the most pertinent one is given the context. Consider, for instance, its treatment of the verb *saber*, which means both *to know* and *to taste*. In relation to a sip of coffee, the obvious choice would be *to taste*, but GT went for *to know*. Can it be true that no one ever

....

5. Jorge Luis Borges, "Word-Music and Translation," *This Craft of Verse* (Cambridge and London: Harvard University Press, 2000), 68.

6. David Bellos, "Automated Language-Translation Machines," *Is that a Fish in Your Ear? Translation and the Meaning of Everything* (New York: Faber and Faber, 2011), 247-258.

translated the phrase "*antes de que supiera amargo*" before, referring to the coffee before it acquired a bitter taste? That said, GT's mistaken inference produced a line that is not devoid of charm and a certain trueness: "One sip of coffee before I *knew* bitter." It signals phenomenological awareness by fusing the perception of an object's qualities with their perceiver, and pointing to the fact that the taste of coffee is not per se unpleasant, but only in the estimation of the one sipping it.

When there is ambiguity as to the subject of a sentence, GT's translations are skewed toward the first person. In that same construction cited above, the conjugation of the verb *supiera* in Spanish would allow for the subject of the sentence to be the first or third person singular. GT, predictably, assigned the tasting to an *I*.

GT translates sequentially, from one syntactical unit to another. It is for this reason that it cannot deduce meaning from what comes after a unit it has already converted to the target language.

Complicating matters, GT has short-term memory only, and therefore scrambles agreement and adjective order.

GT is indifferent to stylistic conventions, as evinced by the lines "A hole in a hole" and "Two paths to a path." It incurs in the type of repetition avoided in so-called well-written texts by the usage of synonyms and the display of a rich vocabulary.

In addition, GT is male-centered and tone deaf. Eyes cannot just be shut while napping; they must belong to a male, and children or offspring must all be sons. In Spanish, if the eye misses accents, questions without question marks cannot be identified. Hence the question "*Cuántos espejos son dos*" (how many mirrors are two?)— implied only by the accent over the *á* differentiating the word from *many* (*cuantos* without an accent) becomes the winning "Many mirrors are twofold."

GT, not unlike the worst translators, is also prone to providing unnecessary elucidations of what it fails to understand in a rather simple or clear text. Since evenings cannot fall and lights cannot just appear out of the blue, it introduces the subject seeing them. The line "Evening falls and two lights appear" therefore becomes "Late afternoon and see two lights." In the third stanza, instead of a comma, it introduces *or* between "an accomplice" and "an enemy" since, given that the terms are opposites, it deems it a contradiction for someone to be both simultaneously. GT misses the point the line seeks to underscore: that from the perspective of a subject in a group of three individuals, one of the other two will be an accomplice of the first, and the third one, an enemy.

Finally, again, not unlike dangerously inept translators who, in Walter Benjamin's characterization, practice the "inaccurate transmission of an inessential content,"[7] GT fails to read those smaller words on which sense tends to rest disproportionately, perhaps: pronouns and prepositions. GT failed to take note of the self-reflexive nature of the question in the fifth stanza: "If five times you ask yourself, / What am I doing here…" simply becomes "And if you ask five times / What am I doing here."

GT = Defamiliarization 101. The estrangement the omission of the reflexive pronoun introduced is more than welcome since it rids the stanza of its heavy dose of self-involvement and it signals the subject's disorientation more genuinely.

GT's output is inventive in that it cannot simply replicate existing discourse ad nauseam, but invariably mangles it, and in doing so, introduces a generative swerve.

. . . .

7. Walter Benjamin, "The Task of the Translator," *Illuminations*, trans. Harry Zohn (New York, Schocken, 1969), 70.

T5:   On "The Poem Is Titled Equivalencies"

Grand Street, Williamsburg. Jane and I sit on the stairwell and play a call-and-response game. When, exactly, I cannot remember. Why.

Location location. Whole Foods has yet to come to the old giant shell on Bedford Ave. where for at least a decade nothing ever happened except large gatherings to which members of the Hassidim community were bussed.

I've already lost a bet that Starbucks won't come to the neighborhood.

The Apple store around the corner hasn't even been conceived. King's Pharmacy is there, but will be forced to close soon, when Duane Reade opens across the street. "Best music in a drugstore ever."

The Mexican bakery where they sold quinceañera cakes has already closed, after their rent was jacked up to $12,000. The steakhouse that'll go on that same corner hasn't opened yet: it'll be called Charcoal + Smoke, or is it Salt + Charcoal, or the other way around. What wasn't branded then is harder to recall and there will be many more displacements to follow.

T6:   On "Equivalent Equivalence"

On September 19, 1923, an excerpt of a letter by Alfred Stieglitz was published in *The Amateur Photographer* under the title "How I Came to Photograph Clouds." He writes: "I wanted to photograph clouds to put down what I had found out in 40 years about photography. Through clouds to put down my philosophy of life—to show that my photographs were not due to subject matter—not to special trees, or faces, or interiors, to special privileges, clouds were there for everyone—no tax as yet on them—free."

Stieglitz's series of cloud photographs is titled *Equivalents* (1925–31). It proposes equivalence between cloud formations and one's fluctuating states of mind. In this sense, clouds are not unlike translations: The process by which one thing becomes akin to another is always already open-ended, never definitive. An equation is an abstraction, and its variables can always be redefined.

Imagine that in one version we only become aware of feeling when looking at clouds and discovering that they mirror what we experience within. In another version, we look for clouds that mirror what we feel and ignore those that don't match. In yet another version, we focus only on those clouds that we can't associate with anything, for they're the true measures of our inwardness and the unpredictability of our moods.

Through photographic alchemy, despite his staunch allegiance to straight photography, Stieglitz converts the ethereal into perceptual objectivity and back, regardless of the nebulosity of his subjects. The *Equivalents* series is a record of our attempts to find correspondences, of our once commonly shared dream to attain spiritual symbiosis with nature. We look up to the sky and we are leveled, made equivalent. The cloud is on demand and available to all.

Imagine this as a form of pathetic fallacy: Cumulus tumble onto the afternoon sky. At sundown, a bed of clouds flares up and turns blood red, before fading into the night.

Hoy el aire no manifestaba ausencia de movimiento aparente—pero lo contrario de la calma tampoco se presentaba de manera visible. Por el momento el cielo se encontraba despejado, pero la inexactitud del pronóstico estaría por verificarse; el día a medias estaba. Se aproximaba un pseudofrente cálido y la troposfera daba la sensación de que se podía tocar. Seis octavos del cielo estaban cubiertos de nubes entrecortadas. La decisión tendría que ser tomada independientemente de las condiciones climatológicas, pues ni siquiera se vislumbraban las implicaciones de interiorizar un cielo aborregado, una nube pared, o una nube en coma. Ni hablar de una nube de escombros. Se encontraría en rotación ciclónica hiciera lo que hiciera y la microrráfaga estaba por comenzar. Del cielo poco le llovería.

T7 & T14:   On "Like in Valencia" and "Equivalence"

Homophonic and homographonic translations are records of the mind's inability to succumb to utter incomprehension and proof of analogical reasoning. It would be difficult to imagine a text whose sonic patterns or visual appearance would be so foreign and indecipherable to someone that it'd completely prevent them from associating it with something known. Most texts and utterances have elements that lend themselves to be compared with something else, forced or mistaken as the correspondences may be.

Anyone who's ever played the game dictionary, or guessed the meaning of obscure words, knows that the larger the discrepancy between one's conjecture and what something actually means, the more humor it produces. Tripping up cognition, be it analog or digital, results in commensurate giddiness.

As much as devices may be bent on eliminating verbal incomprehension from our experience as citizens of the global world, speech-recognition technology frequently gets things wrong. Rapidly evolving software continues to produce reliably erroneous results, especially when faced with idiosyncratic speech patterns and cases of disfluency (stammering; stopping mid-sentence and restarting multiple times; using *ums*, *ahs*, and *likes* frequently; etcetera). In 2012 one of every four words in arbitrary speech was misrecognized,[8] yet by 2017 Google transcribed only one in twenty words mistakenly.[9] This rate is attributable to the implementation of a model replicating the way that neural networks function in the human brain. Phonemes and patterns of consonants and vowels are picked up and classified, and, subsequently, used to make more "sophisticated guesses" as to which words are being said.[10]

"Like in Valencia" and "Equivalence" test these notions and compare an actual brain at work with its machine-operated simulation, or

. . . .

8. According to a video of a live demonstration of Microsoft's neural network-based voice processing software in Tianjin, China, by Microsoft's Chief Research Officer Rick Rashid in October of 2012, included in the article "How Google Retooled Android With Help From Your Brain" by Robert McMillan, Wired.com, February 18, 2013.

9. https://venturebeat.com/2017/05/17/googles-speech-recognition-technology-now-has-a-4-9-word-error-rate/ Searched on Aug. 7, 2019.

10. McMillan, Robert, *Op. cit.*

analog versus digital performance, so to speak. Both originated from a spoken version of "Equivalencias." For the first speech-recognition test, I read the poem out loud and engaged in a call-and-response exercise with a close listener who, except for a very restricted number of words, understands no Spanish at all.

Like in Valencia

<u>cognates</u>

<u>correctly recognized terms</u>

shared phonetic sequence

<u>loosely homophonic terms</u>

<u>false friends</u>

Uno. Un <u>silencio</u>, una <u>llamarada</u>.

The <u>silence</u> of <u>Esmeralda</u>.

*Un **<u>sorb</u>**o de <u>café</u> antes de que **sup**iera amargo.*

The **<u>sorbet</u>** at the <u>café</u> is **sup**erior.

*Un <u>hoyo</u> **dent**ro de un agujero.*

The <u>oil</u> at the **dent**ist was relaxing.

*<u>Dos caminos</u> para una **traj**ectoria.*

The two <u>roads</u> were <u>doubly</u> **trag**ic.

Y sus ojos <u>cerrados</u> durmiendo la <u>siesta</u>.

The <u>serrano</u> peppers caused me to take a long <u>nap</u>.

Cuántos **espe**jos son <u>dos</u>.

The **quant**ity of **spe**ctators was <u>twice</u> as large.

<u>Cae</u> la tarde y aparecen dos luces.

The <u>guy</u> was a little slow on Sunday.

<u>Dos</u> <u>hijos</u> que ya son <u>tres</u>.

The <u>two</u> <u>eels</u> seem like <u>three</u>.

<u>Tres</u> <u>es paz</u> y <u>garantía</u>.

<u>Three</u> <u>in space</u> is <u>guaranteed</u>.

*Un **cómpl**ice, un enemigo.*

Whoever is **compl**acent with me is my friend.

*Tres libros abiertos. Tres **gran**os de sal.*

Three books that have beards. Look **gran**d in the sun.

Cuatro veces dije un nombre, y nada.

Four as a number is nothing.

Cuatro es lo mismo que dos.

Four amuses two.

Y si cinco veces te preguntas…

Five is a vessel.

¿Qué hago aquí?

Something to do with water; water is the key to five.

Quema tu cama, déjala arder, y vete.

Camel to camel, they like to eat green.

The listener is not unique in that he recognizes some of those few Spanish words that most American monolinguals are bound to know (numbers and the word *siesta*, for instance), but his knowledge goes somewhat beyond. Judging from his acquaintance with the noun *camino* (*road*, *path*, or *trail*), we can surmise that he's familiar with the place names particular to territories that were former Spanish colonies, such as California, whose historic trail, the Camino Real, traverses from Sonoma to San Diego.

If the listener's Spanish vocabulary is not extensive, however, his responses to the prompts give us ample evidence of his finely tuned ear. He was able to detect shared phonetic sequences over and over in fragments of words that he then completed in English, producing a rather imaginative record of his mis- or half-understanding (*enemigo* is heard as *amigo* and results in *friend*, *vete* is misunderstood as *verde* and hence leads to *green* in the poem's last line). When he was unable to do that, the listener picked up the sound patterns in the Spanish and transposed them to English, linking words that are unrelated in both languages, including *llamarada* and *Esmeralda*, *veces* and *vessel*, and *cama* and *camel*. Overall, the listener's utterances differed from homophonic translations in that his failure to understand was paired with a willingness to make out what he was hearing regardless, generating not gibberish but rather absurdist statements displaying a compelling tension between plausibility and nonsense.

For the second case, "Equivalence," I read the poem into the GT app on my device, then an iPhone 5. The results were hardly as advanced as the ones above. The fact that the app required to first transcribe the text and then translate it into English accounts for the extreme randomness of the results; many more than one in seven or eight words seem to be wild guesses on GT's part. The inference that what the speaker of the poem said somehow related to *Don Quixote*—given that, like Cervantes's novel, it too had been written in Spanish—flatters the work and beckons Borges and his forgiving approach to translation. Contrary to what authors and readers hold as an article of faith when it comes to editions and translations, in "The Superstitious Ethics of the Reader," from 1931, Borges equates preciousness in a literary text with its precariousness, reassuring us that: "the page that becomes immortal can traverse the fire of typographical errors, approximate translations, or inattentive or erroneous readings without losing its soul in the process. One cannot alter with impunity any line fabricated by Góngora (according to those who restore his texts), but Don Quixote wins posthumous battles against his translators and survives each and every careless version."[11]

It is characteristically sly of Borges to have imperviousness to error act as guarantor of the text's afterlife, and even more so to bring up the translators of *Don Quixote*, since the first one appears in the novel, and thus is entirely fictional. The narrator claims that the book he has been recounting up to chapter eight has abruptly come to an end, and that the story has been able to continue only due to his serendipitous encounter with a purveyor of rare books and manuscripts in a market. One such manuscript contained the novel's alleged Arabic original, by Cide Hamete Benengeli, whose translation the narrator commissions. From that moment on, whenever something doesn't sit well with the novel's narrator, he reliably blames the translator.

....

11. Weinberger, *Op. cit.*, 54.

An Aside on Cervantes and Translation

Miguel de Cervantes, a master at creating intricate, polyphonic labyrinths of fictions within fictions within fictions, was a veteran of the Battle of Lepanto (1571) waged by the Holy League, an alliance of the Spanish Empire, the Venetian Republic, and other maritime powers against the spread of Islam across Western Europe. A harquebus shot had deprived Cervantes's left hand of mobility, which earned him the unfortunate nickname of *El manco de Lepanto* (the Cripple of Lepanto). If the Spanish Golden Age was golden for its letters, these didn't exclude some of the highest examples of epistolary vitriol ever spilled, by writers such as Lope de Vega, for example. In a letter about Lope's snide invectives against him, *Don Quixote*'s author famously wrote: "What I cannot not resent is being singled out for being an old man and a cripple, as if by hand I could stop time, so it could pass me over, or as if my condition had been born in a tavern instead of on the highest occasion that past and present centuries had seen and coming ones can expect to see. [...] If I were granted an impossible request today, I would want to find myself in that prodigious confrontation again and not healthy of my limbs without having participated in it."

One wonders if the author of a biography of Cervantes from 1800, Juan Antonio Pellicer y Pilares, was being hyperbolic when arguing that "wounds [from the Battle of Lepanto] were so cherished, that they were shown off as trophies, with some even willing to pay money for them." So marked was Cervantes by the crusade against the Ottomans and the memento it perpetually left him with—his mangled arm both an award and a ruin of sorts—that the loss of a hand became a recurrent motif in *Don Quixote*. In the novel's prologue, Cervantes claims to transcribe a friend's pragmatic, if irreverent, advice on how to deal with all the perfunctory conventions around dedications, epigrams, and poems by distinguished figures that authors were required to cite prior to putting forth their own literary works: Why not write the material himself and then attribute it to whomever he chooses, if the consequences of being caught falsifying them would be negligible? The friend's reasoning is that should "certain pedants and university graduates backbite and gossip about the truth of the attributions, you should not give two *maravedí* coins for what they say, because even if they prove their falsehood, it's not like they will cut off the hand with which you wrote them."

The useless limb's phantom appears again in chapter nine, with the startling prospect of the retelling of Don Quixote's adventures being left truncated. To the narrator's chagrin and confusion, the story he has been recounting suddenly stops. He wonders how it could be that this knight-errant lacked a wise man by his side to record the entirety of his deeds, as was customary for the other knights in the chivalric romances that he'd read, and admits to not being "inclined to believe that so gallant a history had been left maimed and crippled." The story meets a fate different from that of Cervantes's. It is able to resume, the narrator tells us, thanks to a lucky coincidence and his own zealous reading habit, ironically mirroring Don Quixote's. In a market in Toledo, the narrator spots a young man trying to sell old manuscripts to a silk merchant. Admittedly being "very fond of reading, even torn papers in the streets," he picks up one of the folios, written in Arabic. Upon asking a Moorish passerby to translate a passage into Castilian, the narrator discovers, lo and behold, that it is the continuation of the very story he's been recounting, chronicled by the Arabic historian Cide Hamete Benengeli. From that point on, *Don Quixote* is presented as the translation of the book penned by the fictional and somewhat caricaturized historian, whose name is a spoof on the word *berenjena* (Spanish for *eggplant*).

In the prologue, anticipating postmodernism's obfuscation of authorship, Cervantes introduces himself as the novel's stepfather, not its father. He has allegedly only *adopted* a narrative dreamed up by the Moorish scholar. The distancing conceit, oddly lending *Don Quixote* legitimacy and undermining it at the same time, could not have been more subversive at the time, coming from someone who considered it the highest honor to fight in the Battle of Lepanto, and who subsequently was held captive in Algiers for five and a half years—and especially considering the historical context in which the first part of *Don Quixote* was published, in 1605.

Although anti-Muslim sentiment had been strong in the first half of the sixteenth century, through the payment of a hefty monetary sum to King Charles V, Spain's Moorish population, forced to convert to Christianity, had been afforded a period of relative tolerance in terms of dress and the use of Arabic. By 1567, however, the edict had expired, and with Phillip II at the throne, using Arabic language, dress, and names—not to mention observing Islam—was banned under penalty of death. Chaos and the War of the Alpujarras ensued. As reprisal, the Moorish population was evicted from Granada and dispersed throughout Castilian Spain. Many Moors relocated to La Mancha, whose name in *Don Quixote* is meant as a pun—a *mancha* is *stain* in Spanish, although the place-name comes from the Arabic *al-mansha*, meaning *dry land*—and to the province of Toledo, where the novel's narrator claims to have found Benengeli's manuscript.

The unintended consequence of the relocation of the Moorish population was a rekindling of the Muslim faith among more or less assimilated groups, which, in turn, led Phillip II to decree their definitive expulsion from Spain in 1609. Book burning was part of the purge. About 80,000 books and manuscripts in Arabic were destroyed. Anachronism notwithstanding, had Cide Hamete Benengeli's original not been fictional, it would have met the same fate as these banned books.

Cervantes's radical metafictions run counter to his professed militant fervor. At the heart of the preeminent modern novel is a detonator against fundamentalism that refuses deactivation. It is an understatement to characterize as blasphemous the fact that *Don Quixote*, Spain's most canonical of literary masterpieces, purports itself to have been written by a figure whose very presence in the Spanish empire was contested by the crown, in a language that shortly after the book's publication would be forbidden to speak in public. Cervantes had been a prisoner of war. What did he have to lose by engaging in literary transgressions? It is not like the crown would have cut off his hand for writing seditious fiction built on the ruins of absolutes and shattered symbols. We need not look further than the author's immobilized left hand, both a war trophy and reminder of the body's vulnerability and impermanence, as an emblem of the baroque era's shiftiness and genius at the art of simulation.

To this art we owe the novel and its eschewing of censorship. Was *Don Quixote* even Cervantes's? Another Don Quixote appeared in Alfonso Fernández de Avellaneda's apocryphal sequel, which preceded the real second part of the novel by one year and gave Cervantes enough time to fold in the publication of the fake *Don Quixote* into his own sequel, as well as Don Quixote and Sancho the opportunity to compare themselves with their counterfeit versions. Just like billing something a translation creates the impression of there being an original, that they were imperfectly replicated only strengthened the illusory existence of these fictional characters.

A form of chiaroscuro—that which is illuminated appears all the more real when in contrast with something obscured.

. . . .

Sources for "An Aside on Cervantes and Translation"

Cervantes, Miguel de. *Don Quixote.* Trans. Edith Grossman. New York: Harper Perennial, 2005.

Mayans y Siscar, Gregorio. *Vida de Miguel de Cervantes Saavedra.* London: J. & R. Tonson, 1737.

Pellicer y Pilares, Juan Antonio. *Vida de Miguel de Cervantes Saavedra.* Madrid: Gabriel de Sancha, 1800.

Stone, Robert S. "Moorish Quixote: Reframing the Novel." *Cervantes: Bulletin of the Cervantes Society of America* 33.1 (Spring 2013): 81-112.

T8:   On "Picture Character"

An early draft of the translation, originally titled "Caution!" and later revised.

Venice, May 10, 2019.
After Antoine Catala's installation in the Venice Biennale's Arsenale.

A rebus in the form of a sculptural display with words made of things and things made of words. Its parts awkwardly joined, inviting viewers to translate non-alphabetical signs into a phrase: the anticipation of a spectacle in the form of crowd control ropes is *the* (definite article) + a hologram of a palpitating anatomical heart + an *a* (the letter or indefinite article) imprinted on an inflatable pillow of sorts, gasping for air, emptying itself out and filling itself back up, just like articles do + a group of identical varsity sweaters, most likely found, each with the image of a pink trophy on the front = THE HEART A-TROPHIES.

I wasn't expecting to find our atrophied heart in this former military arsenal still policed by soldiers, since what it stores is incalculably more valuable than armament. Regardless, I manage to steal it.

A wholeness of feeling is what I am after. My parts pull in different directions and resist narrative articulation. And so it is that here I find a longing displayed. I'm assuming you wouldn't arrive at the diagnosis if you didn't feel the heart's progressive decline.

But atrophy equals numb. A stoppage of growth or development, a withering away. Not only does it have nothing to do with heartache, it's probably its opposite, signaling a stunted capacity to feel, among other things, pain.

Emojis magnify feeling and supplant it at the same time, as if its very exaggeration was the key to its surface quality and ultimate riddance. All a matter of ratios.

My heart got stuck in a late-nineties structure of feeling, back when the engineering of desire wasn't as ubiquitous as computing is now.

People eye each other as they eye the art and themselves, but missed connections were numerous given the scale of the fair's many spectacles.

Our dissociation mirrored and multiplied by a generalized scopophilia and this continuing of ourselves as image.

T9:   On "Your Turn"

Concrete Mix. *Gutai* is *concrete* in Japanese. GT proposes other alternatives that include *tangible, material, dense, firm, physical, solid, strong, compressed, hard,* and *compact.*

Concrete in English brings *specific, particular, existing,* and *actual* to the mix, in contrast with abstract. Its etymological origins, per Merriam Webster, are found in the Latin *concrescere* or "to grow together." No examples for this use of *concrete* are instantly locatable, but knowing that grammarians first applied it "to words that expressed a quality viewed as being united with the thing it describes" brings welcome disambiguation. As much as concrete poems and emojis, onomatopoeias aspire to this brand of concreteness.

"Your Turn" is not a concrete poem, but it aspires to Gutai. Its matter, issued forth by the ghost in the machine, is left unaltered.

A Koan: "Out of nowhere, the mind comes forth."

"When matter remains intact and exposes its characteristics, it starts telling a story and even cries out. To make the fullest use of matter is to make use of the spirit," writes Yoshihara Jirō in "Gutai's Art Manifesto" of 1956.[12]

The ghost opens the catalogue of the exhibition *Gutai: Splendid Playground* at the Guggenheim in New York to a page with an image of Yoshihara Jirō standing in front of one of his *Circle* paintings. As the premise for his canvases, it repeats over and over. No circle is ever the same.

Goethe envisions a circle when considering the highest form of translation, one that retains what is foreign in a foreign-language text. One allowing for a circling back to the source, one standing in its place but not replacing it: "The circle, within which the approximation of the foreign and the familiar, the known and the unknown constantly move, is finally complete."

Centrifugal and centripetal drives are contained and in perpetual motion in a figure with no beginning and with no end.

"A circle does what a circle does best." (Bill Callahan)

....

12. Ming Tiampo and Alexandra Munroe, eds. Jirō, Yoshihara, "Gutai Art Manifesto," trans. by Reiko Tomii, *Gutai Splendid Playground*, (New York: Guggenheim Museum Publications, 2013), 18-19.

T10:   On "Same As It Ever Was"

The thrill of identification with Gen X's sensibility.

Dissociation:

"You may find yourself in another part of the world… Well, how did I get here?" (Talking Heads, "Once in a Lifetime," 1982)

"Who's that girl? ¿Quién es esa niña? Señorita tan fina… " (Madonna, "Who's that girl?", 1987)

Spanish infiltrating a provincial monolingualism:

"Soy un perdedor… I'm a loser baby, so why don't you kill me?" (Beck, "Loser," 1994)

Did I really hear that?

MOVIEFONE 777-FILM

Y tu mamá también. (Dir. Alfonso Cuarón, 2001)

Amores perros. (Dir. Alejandro González Iñárritu, 2000)

T11:   On "Self-Mastery"

A ludibrious translation riffing off a pamphlet on Rosicrucianism, enigmatically designated by one of the religious sect's founders, Johann Valentin Andreae, as a "ludibrium" in 1616.

Seeing a solar eclipse (never directly) at the Egyptian Museum at Rosicrucian Park in San José, CA, on August 21, 2017 prompted this translation. The occasion would be particularly auspicious, we were told. As the northern hemisphere became engulfed in the shadow cast by the moon gradually covering the sun, we'd be able to tap into spiritual powers lying dormant within us. If I allowed Rosicrucian language to eclipse the language of the original "Equivalencias," would I discover the poem's hidden mysticism? What symbols lay hidden in the poem?

Erik Satie was a member of the Mystical Order of the Rose and Cross, a Rosicrucian salon frequented by Symbolist artists, writers, and musicians, before founding a new sect, of which he remained the single follower, in 1893. The same year, he wrote the score for *Vexations,* a piece suggesting that the performer play the same musical theme 840 times in succession.

Walking my dog Shadow, I look up to the church kitty-corner from the dog run. A sign outside urges congregants to "Intensify the Work of Propagation." I once heard David Antin define a poem as a "commercial that isn't selling anything." I later encountered this phrase in many of his writings.

If a poem is an ad for language (attentive reading enables you to access a different plane of reality, reach unforeseen levels of feeling and thought) then a translation is an ad for the worldview and sensibility inherent in a foreign language.

T12:   On "Equanimity"

In soccer, one team's wrongdoings might translate into advantages for
the opposing team, among them being awarded free kicks that make
it easier to penetrate the opposing team's defense and score goals.
Hence, causing or claiming the infringement of rules plays a strategic
role in the game, especially since the adoption of the Video Assisted
Referee system in 2016. While so much consideration is granted
to potential and actual infractions, those systemic violations taking
place outside the pitch tend to go unnoticed, however. This becomes
especially pronounced every four years when the FIFA World Cup™
rekindles patriotic sentiment and the performance of national teams
promote the suspension of grievances against the political establish-
ments of spectators' respective countries as well as against the tourna-
ment's governing body.

During the final game of the 2018 World Cup, in which France
defeated Croatia 4-2, four members of Pussy Riot dressed up as cops
and invaded the pitch mid-game to make human rights violations in
the host nation visible among live spectators and TV viewers alike.
"Perhaps you know that there is no rule of law in Russia…" is how
the YouTube video in which they claim responsibility for the action
begins its address to its viewers. Astonishingly, the alien invaders
were able to infiltrate the security apparatus, yet once they were in
action, they were swiftly removed from the pitch, the cameras barely
following them.

catorce
cinco
cuatro
dieciséis
diecinueve
dieciocho
diecisiete
diez
doce
dos
nueve
ocho

eighteen
eleven
fifteen
five
four
fourteen
nine
nineteen
one
seven
seventeen
six
sixteen

once
quince
seis
siete
trece
tres
uno
veinte
veinticinco
veinticuatro
veintidós
veintritrés
veintiuno

**ten
thirteen
three
twelve
twenty
twenty-five
twenty-four
twenty-one
twenty-three
twenty-two
two**[13]

13. In the essay "Irreducible Strangeness," Rosmarie Waldrop writes: "Translation's ultimate task may be to bear witness to the *essentially* irreducible strangeness and distance between languages—but its immediate task is exactly to explore this space." Reprinted in Rosmarie and Keith Waldrop's *Keeping/ the window open: Interviews, statements, alarms, excursions.* (Seattle: Wave Books, 2019), 143-146.

T15:   On "Llamaradas Are Blow Jobs"

Go ahead, I'm listening. I don't understand what you mean by "Camaradas are blow jobs." How about a web search for it? Here's what I found: Madonna Promises Blow Jobs for Hillary Clinton Voters.

Here's what I found: Multipath routing.

I can help you find restaurants if you turn on Location Services. You can also try Wikipedia Chicken Fingers.

Here's what I found: Smart silk dressings—for treating chronic wounds—Atlas of Science.

Sorry, I'm still not sure about that.

I found this on the web: 3 an Apple a Day How to take a screenshot on your Windows 10 Surface device.

Sorry, I'm still not sure about that.

Could you restate the question? It's about 4/3 = 1.3333.

I don't know where you are, Monica. But you can help me find out by turning on Location Services. Or you can just tell me where to check the weather.

I found this on the web: How Are Criminal Charges Filed? How Fines and Fees Criminalize Poverty.

I'm not sure I understand.

I found this on the web: Mother Trying to Help Son Find a Date Draws Complaints.

Here are some Thor picks: Avengers: Infinity Wars, Avengers:

Endgame.

I didn't find any appointments on August 3, 2020.

Interesting question, Monica.

Tip: Curious about what I can do? Just ask "what can you do?" or say "help."

What's showers in Spanish? *Duchas*.

Sure, translate into which language? Arabic, German, Spanish, French, Italian, Japanese, Brazilian Portuguese, Russian, Mandarin Chinese. I can't translate into Croatian yet.

I can't translate into Us resist questions yet.

I don't know how to respond to that.

Well, since a woodchuck is really a groundhog, the correct question would be: "How many pounds in a groundhog's mound when a groundhog pounds hog mounds?"

T16:   On "Equivocation"

The ghost in the machine is fond of radical code-switching. Despite its being an incongruous assemblage of random terms, interjections, and bastardization of both English and Spanish, its translation retains communicability, proving the poem's resilience.

Perhaps the holes in the poem's associative logic make it especially open and porous. As a performance text it produces, Dada-like, playful guttural sounds pleasing to the tongue producing them and to the ear receiving them.

"Ina llama dada" is a particularly good example of productive ambiguity given that the text could be read in Spanish or English and yield two different meanings. After a solemn interjection, appears:

Ina, the dada llama (as in the pack animal in the family of camels and particular to region of the Andes)

or

Ina (a proper name) and a given flame (if the phrase is read in Spanish)

Turning "Cuántos espejos son dos" (*How many mirrors are two*) into "Chanting selenide" seems absurd until you discover that both phrases relate to optical phenomena: selenide gives quantum dots, used in nanotechnology, distinctive spectral qualities. (Quantum dots emit fluorescence on excitation with a light source.)

Among the ghost's astute swerves are:

Turning *libros* (books) into *libido*, suggesting the erotics of the book

cómplice (accomplice) into *compile*, as in legal evidence,

enemigo (enemy) into *evenly*, underlining the reciprocity of enmity,

110

nombre (name) into *bomb*, underscoring the violence of naming,

si (if) into *CIA*, pointing to the way investigations proceed via hypotheticals,

mismo (same) turns into *gizmo*, both similarly unspecific and only differentiated when alongside the thing they're equal to,

que (that, what, which, how) into *queer* or *queen*, signaling its non-conformity with gender, *que* being a gender-fluid relative pronoun,

veces (times) into *vexes* for, yes, it is vexing to have to keep asking,

déjala (leave her alone) into *female*, signaling a feminist awareness,

vete (the command to leave) into *veteran*, suggesting it might be time to dash.

T17:   On "Birdwatching"

A poetics manifesto and a translation creed, Vallejo's *Trilce* XXXVI is a statement against correspondence—it's anti-Symbolist at its core. Throughout *Trilce*, expression reaches such a degree of idiosyncrasy and differentiation that it's as if Vallejo had written some of the poems in a private language.

In the essay "Variations on the Right to Remain Silent," Anne Carson argues that the one way out of commonplace and cliché is catastrophe: "We resort to cliché because it's easier than trying to make up something new."[13] Neologisms stand for the sign's catastrophe. They're at the edge of a known language, sounding the limits of the expressible. They're untranslatable. *Trilce*. Hölderlin's *pallaksch*.

Most of the poems in Vallejo's *Trilce* dwell in that liminal zone. Nonetheless, I found myself wanting each word and idiomatic phrase in my translation to correspond to the original, to be its equivalent. A more fitting approach would have attempted the opposite—it would have been noncompliant, insubordinate. Then again, a more appropriate translation would have complied with Vallejo's call to refuse symmetry, and in that sense it would have been obedient, agreeable. A catch-22.

The etymology of *harmony* according to the Merriam Webster: "Middle English *armony*, from Anglo-French *armonie*, from Latin *harmonia*, from Greek, joint, harmony, from *harmos* joint—more at ARM.

TRILCE XXXVI

    (*A translation for Miguel de Cervantes*)

We strive to go through a needle's eye
at loggerheads, bent on winning.
The circle's fourth angle almost ammoniafies itself.
The male going on female, due to

....

13. Anne Carson, *Nay Rather* (Center for Writers & Translators, The American University of Paris & Sylph Editions, 2013), 10.`

probable breasts, and precisely
due to that which won't bloom!
Are you there, Venus of Milo?
You're barely impaired
entrailed within the plenary arms
of existence,
of this existence stillhoisting
perennial imperfection,
Venus of Milo, whose severed, un-created
arm twists and tries to elbow itself
through greening gurgling pebbles,
rising nautili, yets that have just
started crawling, immortal eves.
Lassoer of the imminent, lassoer
of parentheses.

Refuse, and you as well, to set foot
on the twofold security of Harmony.
Refuse symmetry for sure.
Intervene in the conflict
of ends battling
in the most heated of jousts
to leap through the needle's eye!

And so I feel my pinky
as an add-on to my left hand. I see it and suppose
it is not me, or at least that it is
where it shouldn't be.
And this enrages me and vexes me
and there's no way out, except pretending
that today is Thursday.

Yield to the new odd
                    potent with orphanhood!

T18: On "Updated Prior Inscription"

"Birdwatching" suggests a path toward asymmetry and noncompliance. "Updated Prior Inscription" is its execution—a disjointed translation infiltrated by the foreign and non-germane to the subject. One that resists the policing of the transfer of meaning. It refuses one-to-one correspondence as well as narrow notions of equivalence by welcoming non-normative meanings, the ones that theoretically do not fit the context. Predictably, the authorities show up. As for borders, where does a poem begin and another end?

T19:   On "A Big, Beautiful Wall"

About a third of the translations of "Equivalencias" were completed
during a residency at the Montalvo Arts Center in Saratoga, California,
in 2017 and 2018, located near the heart of Silicon Valley. It was eerie
to be in such proximity, and physically oriented in relation to, the tech
corporations whose platforms and services have become inextricable
from everyday life. Montalvo's grounds are less than twenty miles away
from Googleplex, Google's corporate headquarters, and less than ten
miles away from Apple's, in Cupertino.

The techno-utopianism so emblematic of both corporations is in
sharp contrast with the region's labor and migration history, a frag-
ment of which is encapsulated in the history of Villa Montalvo itself.
In Wikipedia it is described as follows:

> "Located amidst a 175-acre natural landscape, Villa Montalvo
> was built by the late Senator James D. Phelan in 1912. Upon
> his death in 1930, the Senator gifted his beloved estate to the
> San Francisco Art Association to be maintained 'as a public park
> [with] the buildings and grounds immediately surrounding... to
> be used as far as possible for the development of art, literature,
> music, and architecture by promising students.'"

James D. Phelan (1861–1930), the son of an Irish immigrant, was
Mayor of San Francisco from 1897–1902 and Democratic senator
from 1915–21. He ran an unsuccessful reelection campaign for sena-
tor on the slogan "Keep California White." He supported the Chinese
Immigration Act of 1882 and his work with the Japanese Exclusion
League of California led to the Immigration Act of 1924, which
banned Arabs and virtually all Asians from immigrating to the United
States. He was a conservationist whose views on the environment fol-
lowed a nativist rationale. In the invective "Why California objects to
the Japanese Invasion" (1921), he wrote: "We must preserve the soil
for the Caucasian race."

Phelan echoed the white supremacist views of Madison Grant and
his disciples (as can be seen in "The False Pride of Japan," a letter sent

to the editors of *The Atlantic* in response to a contribution by Henry W. Kinney). The immigration quotas in the Immigration Act of 1924, in fact, were based on Madison Grant's eugenicist writings. His volume *The Passing of the Great Race* (Scribner's, 1916) is prefaced by Henry Fairfield Osborn, Professor of Zoology at Columbia University, thus:

> "History is repeating itself in America at the present time and incidentally is giving a convincing demonstration of the central thought in this volume, namely, that heredity and racial predisposition are stronger and more stable than environment and education [...] the Anglo-Saxon branch of the Nordic race is again showing itself to be that upon which the nation must chiefly depend for leadership, for courage, for loyalty, for unity and harmony of action, for self-sacrifice and devotion to an ideal. Not that members of other races are not doing their part, many of them are, but in no other human stock which has come to this country is there displayed the unanimity of heart, mind and action which is now being displayed by the descendants of the blue-eyed, fair-haired peoples of the north of Europe. [...]" (Second edition, 1917)

Grant's was a "capital book" according to Theodore Roosevelt's blurb for it, one that showed "a fine fearlessness in assailing the popular and mischievous sentimentalists and attractive and corroding falsehoods which few men dare assail." This was a book "all Americans should be sincerely grateful" for, in Roosevelt's estimation.

Amid verbiage excoriating the "lower or inferior races" that threaten to "replace" the so-called Nordic race, Grant warns readers of the dangers posed, in particular, by miscegenation. In a chapter titled "Language, Ethnicity and Race," he writes:

> "When it becomes thoroughly understood that the children of mixed marriages between contrasted races belong to the lower type, the importance of transmitting in unimpaired purity the blood inheritance of ages will be appreciated at its full value and to bring half-breeds into the world will be regarded as a social and racial crime of the first magnitude."

That it is a platitude to state that indeed history is repeating itself in America does not make this fact less true, less demoralizing, or less alarming. As I was working on my translations in the summer of 2018, the Trump administration implemented a "zero tolerance" approach to migrant families detained at the border, which resulted in the separation of families and the unprecedented detention of more than 2,600 children in government shelters. According to an article published in the *Washington Post* on July 28th, 2018, there was no established category for these families in the Customs and Border Patrol databases, since they no longer constituted "family units" and the minors, having traveled north *with* their parents, were not "unaccompanied alien children." A new category was hence established, that of "deleted families." The situation would only get worse in 2019.

A translator whose identity I would prefer not to remember once told me that I should avoid Latinates if I wanted my translations to come across as artful. The standard was for the works in question to pass as having been written originally "in English," his selective view of the history of the English language notwithstanding.

"A Big, Beautiful Wall" employs only words with an Anglo-Saxon origin and etymology. Banned words include *silence, flames, coffee, mirror*, and *peace*.

T20: On "La más mimética de todas"

"The translator is no stand-in or ventriloquist for the foreign author, but a resourceful imitator who rewrites the original to appeal to another audience in a different language and culture, often in a different period." (Lawrence Venuti, "How to Read a Translation")

To distract the authorities, the resourceful imitator pretended to go off the rails, and smuggled the goods in plain sight.

T21: On "From Mother to Daughter"

In *Wars. Threesomes. Drafts. & Mothers*, Heriberto Yépez describes a procedure called interwriting used occasionally by the narrator of his novel. It consists of finding a passage, interpolating it between periods, and then ditching the original while keeping one's own sentences. If a mother-text has periods then it is able to spawn a new text commenting on it, interpolating it or critiquing it, the narrator's argument goes. A new text replaces and eventually cancels a mother-text that disappears almost without a trace. You could argue that interwriting is a form of translation as well, in which the language of the mother-text is internalized by its offshoot.[14] In any translation, as Brandon Brown has written apropos of radical translations, a preceding text corresponds to a proceeding one. This new one may or may not remain within familiar boundaries and may or may not acknowledge its source. But here, if we are to go along with the procreation metaphor, who plays the text's father then? The child proposed by Yépez's narrator could turn out to be a spitting image of its dad.

I paraphrase but don't quote, interwriting, as it were, though for this version of the poem I did try the procedure. No replacement here, however, the mother-text was mine after all.

My mother just texted me to ask how the book is going. "Hola Mon. Como va el libro?" (Blowing kisses emoji three times.)

14. Heriberto Yépez, *Wars. Threesomes. Drafts. & Mothers* (Factory School, 2007).

T22:   On "Equivocal Valences"

Another procreation metaphor is Cecilia Vicuña's "milk del translate" in
the book *Instan*.[15] It is gentler, not solipsistic, and wildly generative and
imaginative in its linking visual forms and the indigenous and colonial
languages of the Americas through utopian etymologies. They give cre-
dence to Benjamin's idea in "The Task of the Translator" that languages
are not "strangers to one another, but are, *a priori* and apart from all
historical relationships, interrelated in what they want to express." [16]

 As an attempt to avoid the binaries that can often plague bilinguals,
this poem was written around the English-language words embed-
ded in the original. Not all findings were utilized. Spaces between
words in the Spanish version of "*Equivalencias*" were eliminated
and the resulting text was treated as if it were an ambiguous figure,
such as Joseph Jastrow's duck-rabbit, in Wittgenstein's *Philosophical
Investigations*,: "If you search in a figure (1) for another figure (2), and
then find it, you see (1) in a different way."

15   Cecilia Vicuña, *Instan* (Kelsey Street Press, 2002), unpaginated.

16   Benjamin, *Op. cit.*, 72.

unounsilenciounallamarada.
unsorbodecaféantesdequesupieraamargo.
unhoyodentrodeunagujero.

doscaminosparaunatrayectoria
ysusojoscerradosdurmiendolasiesta.
cuantosespejossondos.
caelatardeyaparecendosluces,
doshijosqueyasontres.

tresespazygarantía,
uncompliceunenemigo.
treslibrosabiertostresgranosdesal.
cuatrovecesdijeunnombreynada.
cuatroeslomismoquedos.

ysicincovecesteppreguntas
quéhagoaquiquematucama
déjalaarderyvete.

noun lama rad a
orb decaf ante pie AA go
ho den trod nag

do scam I spar tray or I a
us rad mien la I
ant
CA tar yap are end OS
dos I

res rant I a
comp lice I go
I bros bi OS nos Sal
trove nom
slo –ism

I in Co. step gun
hag IQ mat cam
AA vet

121

T23:   On "Hola, Mi Amor"

A reenactment of the original poem with the same actors, who've switched to English and have gone off script. Some may even be AWOL, literally.

T24:   On "Latin Lover"

Yes, we too can also make repetition new! Inspired by the reenactment leading to "Hola, Mi Amor," the actors in the straightforward translation of "Equivalencias" switch back to Spanish and decide to go off script themselves. Some are said to have gone missing. They title the production in honor of Rudolph Valentino—the Southern Italian silent film actor who after arriving on Ellis Island, went from often-fired bus-boy and gardener, to taxi dancer and exotic gangster, to the antidote to all-American action heroes and heartthrob to women the world over. In search of an audience, though, these poem's actors ultimately agree to being translated.

T25:   On "I was having a flashback."

For Kierkegaard "what is recollected has already been and is thus repeated backwards, whereas genuine repetition is recollected forward."[17] This piece attempts to go back and forth, to generate something out of recollection and repetition.

As in Eliot Weinberger's *19 Ways of Looking at a Wang Wei*, where nineteen different English versions of Wang Wei's original poem in Chinese, titled variously from "Deer Park" to "Deep in the Mountain Wilderness," have the effect of thickening the woods in the poem through which a ray of light enters.[18] It is the light of the original.

As in Eva Hesse's trying a number of different materials when making *Repetition Nineteen* in 1967. There were many do-overs for the nineteen vessels that comprise the piece. They were done three different times as sculptures, and many more times as drawings, so, all in all, *Repetition Nineteen* has many more than nineteen repetitions, if one includes the trials. In 1968, Hesse found the right material: translucent fiberglass, allowing for the passage of light, and assertive of the forms' corporealness. Of these nineteen vessels, some lean sideways, some are slender and some are stocky, some droop, some reach upward. They're all somewhat dented, imperfect, and happily gathered on the floor without a particular order. They seem more interested in assembling than in being on display. They're equivalent, idiosyncratic. Each in their bodies, circling a hollow. They do not mirror each other. Repetition, in their case, lies elsewhere.

Do-overs promise but rarely deliver. Do-overs that deliver don't count as do-overs. They're something else entirely.

· ·

17. Soren Kierkegaard. *Repetition and Philosophical Crumbs*, trans. M. G. Piety (Oxford, UK: Oxford, 2009), 3.

18. Eliot Weinberger & Octavio Paz. *19 Ways of Looking at Wang Wei* (New York: New Directions, 1987).

137 Northeast Regional

Greetings from the future, Jack. You rightly said to Lorca that years down the line I or some other poet might write something corresponding to the letters you addressed to him in *After Lorca*. "That is how dead men write to each other," you declared. I am not a man, but I felt invited to do just that, and I thank you for it.

It's a crisp, radiant autumn day. The landscape is at its peak. Are these words enough to drag the real into the poem? To feel buoyant all I need to do is not get in the light's way. I'm in transit, en route to New York. Translating myself, you could say, in the geometrical sense.

The more I write to you now the more I'm missing seeing the landscape fleet by. I don't even have something to say to you at this time. I'll return to you once the sun has gone down.

Yours,
Mónica

PS: I've been commuting to Providence for over a year and not until now did I get why C.D. Wright sold me on the prospect of being able to do some writing on the train. I've been sitting in the wrong car all these months. The quiet car, where I automatically turn myself into a cop policing people's loud typing and cell-phone use. Do they not know they're sitting in the quiet car? It should be library silent. Don't they get it? (An aside: *Soy una tumba*, "I am a grave," is the Spanish idiom for "my lips are sealed." I just taught David Antin's *Talking*. The introduction has a quote from Antin's essay on Wittgenstein in which he relates how the philosopher stopped lecturing from notes because "the words looked like 'corpses' when he began to read them.")

Here in the café car, tables are solid enough that you don't get dizzy or have to put all your energy into preventing your laptop from sliding from the tray table. You can even look out the window as you type. And since there are no seats compartmentalizing the views further, what you get is expansive, sweeping, glorious.

PPS: Okay, one more thing before I let you keep resting, peacefully, I hope. I adore your notion of single poems not bound to longer sequences or book projects as one-night stands. Monogamy is so hardwired into me, it even regulates my writing. One-offs of all kinds I find too unsettling. That might be the reason why instead of taking the southbound train earlier today I got on the one to Boston. I was in a daze all morning since waking from a dream in which I was about to have an affair with someone who was very handsome and highly masculine; a Latin lover of sorts. In real life I've never met him. Unexamined masculinity I find disconcerting, but what I was most startled by in the dream was the intensity of feeling. Is that how you felt about Lorca? I would have fallen in love with him too had not so many others done so already. I'm more of a cult person. Popularity turns me off. Too predictable. I mean, here I am in the café car speaking to the dead. After I asked the conductor if I was on the wrong train earlier this afternoon, a man turned to me and said, "It's my worst nightmare. Maybe you're in a dream. Maybe all of us here are in your dream." I'm back on track now. Bye for now. Oh, and thank you for reminding me that different types of love are possible.

★

Dear Jack,

I love looking at people looking out the window, lost in thought. It gives you a sense of their interiority. Letters do the same. Take the guy a few tables down, he looks so wistful. He goes from his computer screen to gazing out onto the ocean. This train's route follows the shoreline. I wonder if he's reading about the most recent mass shooting. I couldn't get myself to read the news about it. I feel more outrage than empathy. I want to say I'm starting to become immune, but that'd be a lie, since it's been a gradual, steady atrophy of my ability to sympathize. We get what we deserve, is what I think. (Never thinking myself part of that *we*, which is peculiar, and complicated.) I told you I might get heavy if I kept on writing. Best to go on listening to Radiohead's "Present Tense" instead: "Don't get heavy, keep it light and keep it moving." It's my "self-defense against the present." I'm channeling the lyrics. What kind of music did you like? In this, you're like the people around me listening to something privately, in public. What they're hearing is literally inside their heads and is nothing but a complete mystery to the rest. (Unless they're blasting the music and their earbuds leak sound.)

PS: I thought you'd appreciate knowing that I just passed the Mystic Shipyard. Rocks are beautiful in their resistance to narrative. I just saw a swan!

★

Jack, hi again,

In your correspondence to Lorca you mention a letter you couldn't finish. You write: "You were like a friend in a distant city to whom I suddenly was unable to write [...] because I was suddenly, temporarily, not in the fabric of my life." If I'm responding to the letters Lorca wasn't able to reply to himself, why am I not writing this in Spanish? I doubt he would've chosen to write to you in English. Apropos of friendship, did you know that *fabric* and *fábrica* are false friends? *Fabric* is *tela* and *fábrica* is a factory where things are fabricated, manufactured. It almost seems like you knew this when writing elsewhere: "Nothing matters except the big lie of the personal—the lie in which these objects do not believe."

> Love from the *fábrica* of my life's fabric,
> M.

★

Hello again, Jack,

More than an hour has gone by. The sun hasn't gone down fully yet. There's a heavy swath of gray descending upon a ring of glowing orange. I'm now in Bridgeport, where the landscape has turned industrial. I need your words now, so much less than you need mine. Regarding reciprocity, I wonder if you looked for signs that could be interpreted as Lorca's posthumous responses to your letters. Did you think he'd send you signals from beyond the grave? Now, there's a troubled phrase, especially in this case, since the search for Lorca's remains continues. Forgive me, please.

I see embers in the sky. Splotches of iridescent orange-pink amid the gray. I look up again, but they're gone. How quickly it goes dark.

Love to you,
M.

PS: Chitra, whom I've known since before 9/11, got on the train in New Haven. As it turns out, she studied with C.D. as an undergrad. At the time she fantasized about becoming a poet, but she became a visual artist instead. Her voice warms up when mentioning C.D. What if she were here with us now, in the café car?

PPS: Another odd coincidence: the woman with bright blue nail polish and two cell phones who was sitting across from me leaves, and a new person takes her seat. He too lays two cell phones on the table. C.D., Jack, are you trying to tell me something? Like you, Jack, I wish I could make poems out of real objects.

Thank you for allowing me this public intimacy. You keep haunting these words. You famously wrote, "Words are what sticks to the real. We use them to push the real, to drag the real into the poem." What's the real in *you*? What or whom exactly have I dragged—or translated, in the reanimating sense—into the text? I've reached my destination. Or so I think. For C.D., poetry moves by indirection, and thus "changes the route, and often the destination." I am where I should be. Bye for now, fellow traveler.

Replay

It's the fall of 2017. On the main lawn at the center of Madison Square Park in NYC, a green circular floor or stage, a red pavilion arcade, and a curved and acoustically reflective blue wall comprising Josiah McElheny's Prismatic Park—*a public art project—provide respective settings for dance, poetry, and music performances by artists in residency. The following pages chronicle some of what transpired during my residency there, facilitated by the Madison Square Park Conservancy and Poets House.*

Picture a prism refracting a ray of light and making rainbows. Once it was thought that white light was colorless and that prisms produced the colors they emitted. Later Newton demonstrated that all the colors already existed in the light, and that prisms fanned out the colors of the spectrum because particles of varying hues traveled through them at different speeds. Now imagine that a line of poetry is a ray of light, and that a prism is a translation machine of sorts. You might say something in English, but when you refract it through the prism, a Chinese speaker might pick up on phonemes that mean something else, which in turn differs from what speakers of Arabic, Polish, Spanish, or any other language might be able make out from what they heard.

*

With this in mind, in this series of workshops for Josiah McElheny's *Prismatic Park* at Madison Square Park, we will generate poetry by experimenting with multidirectional translation. Passersby and park visitors—both monolinguals and those fluent in languages other than English—are invited to engage in reciprocal translation experiments, creative mishearing, homophonic and homographonic translation as a way to generate poems that make the most of New York City as a Babel of languages. Poetry, indeed, will be made by all! (As Lautréamont would have it.) Fluency in English decidedly not necessary!

Hoy tengo sólo la suerte suficiente

presente y despierto antes de la primera luz en uno minúsculos
de los establos donde nace el amor ∴ flotan pequeñísimos barcos
a través de la melodía central de la alborada de hoy ∴
pequeños sombreritos blancos, nuevas flores del patio de la
escuela de la iglesia ∴ las hermanas de sus aldeas
the villages sisters,

Magritte & Rosa entre los nuevos brotes, piedras
flameantes/ flameando del volcán de este momento,
¡ joyas ~ bellas!

¿ Dónde están las señoras elegantes que algún día en las
se convertirán?

éste es
el primer fruto de los exuberantes, escondidos pueblos
de las montañas de Puerto Rico. Aquí:

pétalos y flores
aún por florecer, pistilo aún verde oscuro, tallo y hoja

La Noche

aún no entiende estos vehículos/ recipientes.

La noche
posterior   aplastar
tiene diseños en una etapa tardía   para   destruir
romper
estos corazones tiernos,
tal vez.

de ruinas largamente muertas   Fluyen los ríos de la noche
los ríos nocturnos

por ahora, [déjenme] atestiguar en silencio al protector de las
tumbas que se enraíza, dando sombra a un paisaje secreto
a través del lodo recién revolcado, mundo de lagos sepultados/
repletos de ~ antiguas lágrimas de diosa
lágrimas de las cuales (emergirán) brotes nuevamente sembrados,
(erigiéndose) en los frutos y los jardines de Astarté.
Amen, sisters, amen.

A girl and her boyfriend sit at the folding table set up inside the poetry pavilion. Her sports jersey calls out to me. Ukraine, it reads. She's a figure skater for the country's national team and her name is Alina. She corrects the Russian translation of "Poetry will be made by all" in the poster I've placed strategically for people like her to notice it. That is, so that speakers of the languages included in the different translations of the phrase and merely curious passersby can read it.

"Поэзия будет всеми сочинена. It's missing a syllable."

Soon after she's doing handstands on the lawn.

"How do you say that in Russian?" I ask.

"*Stoyka na rukakh.*"

Steven hears "Stoke stack Ruth car."

Yes, she knows Russian poetry. Her mother's told her she'd go around reciting Pushkin as a ten-year-old. She offers the opening lines of "Ruslan and Ludmila" from memory, which I then find translated as:

> By the sea stands a green oak tree
> A golden chain strung around it:
> And on the chain a learned cat
> Day and night circles round it;
> Walking right, he sings a song,
> Walking left, he tells a tale…

She leaves.

*

A youngish man on his lunch break takes Alina's seat with Bolaño's *2666* in hand. His name is LJ and he's a barman at 11 Madison Park.

He'll do a translation experiment with me, sure. I pick a paragraph from the book at random and produce an alternate original. LJ makes out a few bits upon hearing my Spanish version:

From here, we conclude that the Araqueños were:

1. Telepathic.
2. Understood the language of wind through the trees.
3. Travelled all around the world, particularly to India, to old Germany, or to the Peloponnesian Islands.
5. That the Araqueños were incredible mariners.

We leave it at that; his lunch break's over.

*

Trees continue their communication. What if they were using the telepathic language of the Araucanians in *2666* that permitted the indigenous peoples and exiles scattered around globe after Pinochet's coup to communicate amongst each other? We're in the middle of Manhattan but you wouldn't know it except for the skyscrapers surrounding the park. The trees provide shelter but they also transport us elsewhere.

At this time, in the park, there are nannies all around, nannies speaking with other nannies in their mother tongues, busy nannies, focused nannies, their mothering labor complicating the notion of the mother tongue.

I speak with one from Ecuador. The toddler she takes care of, she tells me, knows French, Italian, and Spanish words.... His mother is Rumanian.

"¿Pero cuántos años tiene este niño que habla tantos idiomas?"

"Año dos meses."

"Y su mamá sólo me deja hablar con él en español, para que lo aprenda."

And so she doesn't practice her English as much as she would like to because she's only to speak with the boy in Spanish.

*

It's too hot out. We move away from the sun-blasted pavilion to the shade. Two writing teachers visiting from North Carolina come sit with me: Fran and Barbara. They love New York. They went to a Broadway show. They've heard of Lorca. I read them a part of *"Ciudad sin sueño"* ("A Sleepless City") from *Poeta en Nueva York.*

Fran hears it as:

> Tonight no sleep
> as the moon bathes the city with light
> tomorrow we wake alert
> to the morning clamor and sights

Barbara turns it into:

New Yorka

No one sleeps
Not the young or the old
Or the dogs
Even the dead are awake.

Everyone reads the shadows
Everyone knows.
Disaster is coming
Everyone is aware.

Aux armes, New York!
Aux armes, pour la cité!

"You really picked up on all the death in the poem. Lorca wasn't an 'I love New York" kind of guy."

"Read the original again so we can compare."

I do and then improvise a translation of the excerpt:

the iguanas will come to bite the dreamless men

and the one fleeing with a broken heart

will find in corners   the incredible crocodile, still,
  under the tender protest of the stars

nobody sleeps in the world   nobody
          nobody

a dry landscape on his knee

          we fall down the stairs to eat moist earth

or we go up through the snow with a chorus of dead dahlias

          no oblivion no sleep only live flesh

                    kisses tie mouths into knots of recent veins

                    *

Josiah stops by.

"Do people talk about the weather in Swedish?"

"Oh yes. When you first encounter a new culture, you wonder:
What is culturally different, and how does the language differ? In Sweden
people don't talk much. And they also have a very different idea of indi-
viduality. Like, for instance, people who grew up in the US are all about
patting each other in the back when you meet, like 'Hi, how are you?'"

All go, "Yeah!"

"In Sweden it's like…" he makes a distancing gesture with his
hand, and everybody laughs. "Meaning, 'I wouldn't want to impose

myself on you, so if you want something, I'm here, but I wouldn't want to…' But as I slowly learned to speak better Swedish and spent time in my village for the past thirty or so years, the funny thing I noticed is that, in the end, everybody says the same things everywhere!"

"Really?!"

"Like, the way people talk about the weather, I mean, is exactly the same! It's no different." His laughter is contagious. "There's a famous Swedish word that can't be translated. It's the word *lagom* and it means 'not too much, not too little.' You could apply it to a person. Here we have the concept of a person being too much, but we don't have the concept of a person being too little."

"So what does it mean to be too little?"

"Maybe someone with false humility is too little. Or perhaps someone who's too shy. But *lagom* also means kind of 'enough.' 'I have enough money. I have enough love.' There they have, in every aspect of life, what's a sufficient amount. The idea of the 'good enough' mother is inherently encoded in Swedish culture. Like, basically, with motherhood, you're not expected to be perfect. You're expected to be good enough."

"Wow."

"In English saying 'I've had enough' has a negative charge."

"True. If you give someone a plate of too much food, that's not *lagom*, you gave them too much food."

"It's basically the same principle as 'Give a man a fish, he'll eat for a day. Teach a man to fish, he'll eat forever.'"

A loud collective gasp is heard. Greg reclines in his chair so much he ends up falling on his bum on the muddy ground.

Greg, who has proverbs and quotes at the tips of his fingers, is a cook, chants with the Hare Krishnas, and has witnessed most of today's encounters. Before the day's session wraps up, he writes a chant to resuscitate words from a poster I brought with a list of Spanish terms that have fallen off the language, into disuse.

CHANT TO RAISE DEAD WORDS BACK TO LANGUAGE,
RISING WORDS BACK INTO THE SONG, THEREBY
DUMPING A GOTHAM CITY POET ON HIS ASS INTO A
NEW-TURNED LATE SEPTEMBER PARK MUD

Krita	Indiamina	Jifero	Lalar	
	Melagra	Melagra	Nipos	Melagra
Pulpe	Nuflas Izaga	Leontina		
	Melagra	Melagra	Nipos	Melagra
Oencia	Limalla	Oencia	Limalla	
	Nuco Putamen	Intérlope		
Kemanga				
Jubo Neque	Jubo	Neque		
	Jifero Puquío	Óbice Jofre		
Kora	Juvenco	Kora	Juvenco	
	Lucillo	Pupuso Lucillo Pupuso		
Pupuso				Pupuso

Jabberwocky

Pussy mose sene a saquet
Against may be fed for feast
Some read unidreden
Y la villa grant oit
Mustard ocasi oso
I can't bare it
The bear
Ascuani o deuhe (day) (d e)

Children Freud's friend
From the file, fear not
Ooo la la
Die for lack of breath
Night surround
                    mere
Fear ~~then~~ (existence).
       ^

Anyone who's been in the city long enough knows there's a price to pay for the bounty good weather brings, a steep or negligible one depending on one's sensitivity to construction noise. Today we're trying another spot near the park's north fountain, on what would be 25th Street. A couple shows up. Lew is American, María is from Ecuador.

"At this point I'm more comfortable in English. It's changed through the years."

"How long have you been here?"

"Forty-seven years."

"I have something to show you. Here's this poster with words that are defunct in Spanish."

"They're what?"

"It's words that nobody uses anymore, they're obsolete. Some are cognates, like this one: *intérlope*."

"I don't even know what that means."

"It's related to *interloper*."

"Someone who inserts themselves where they don't belong."

"Yeah, an opportunist."

"I knew somebody named Jofre."

"*Melagro* looks like *milagro*, miracle."

"It does, sí."

"I mean, there are possibilities but no veo algo que pueda decir esto sí sé qué es. *Juvenco* may have something to do with youth. *Ológrafo* sounds like something to do with writing. That comes to mind. Algo que ver con escritura pero no sé qué exactamente."

"Yeah, maybe. No tengo idea. I don't know what a *noema* is either."

"You don't know?" she cackles. "I thought I was supposed to know. I mean, for how long have they not been in use?"

"I'll look it up. Doesn't *inmoto* look familiar?"

"In the mood, in the…"

*

Gregory, not to be confused with yesterday's Greg, shows up with a friend.

"Hey! This is Marit, an artist from Norway."

"Marit, is your name a version of María?"

"No, it's a very old-fashioned Norwegian name."

"So the blue curving, the blue sculpture, is Josiah's?"

"Yeah. What if María from Ecuador and Marit from Norway had the same name?"

"María Dolores, originally."

"With a few other names, of course," interjects Lew, whom I keep referring to as Louie.

"Funny, I don't think the name Dolores has equivalents in other languages."

"When I'm bad sometimes I say 'María *me da* dolores.'"

No one but me gets the joke: María gives him pains. Gregory is more curious than impatient. "So what's going on here?"

"I just read them a piece of mine in Spanish and they each wrote a poem based on what they heard. They have yet to show us what they did. Consider yourselves recruited."

Gregory looks at Lew's cap, "Are you a Yankee's fan?"

"I am."

"Severino was great last night."

"He's their best pitcher. So you want me to read my poem, if I'm not too embarrassed?"

> Ilya, a marauder
> sore bow, calf, a
> pole, yo, olla pot
> smoking hot
> 2 roads diverged in a yellow wood
> Sí, está!

glasses, I spied, holistically
quiet the evening
a child has been added
from 2 to 3
tía guarantees tea
très Lee Bros, I doze
4 x I said a name and
nothing happens until you begin
veer to ti.

"Great! What about your version, María?"

"I wasn't sure what I was supposed to do. I wrote while you were
reading."

Silence Flame A Sip
Un hoyo dentro de un agujero
4   2 lights
1 grandchild
friend & foe
3 open books
No reply - No answer
4 = 2
What am I doing here?
If no answer, burn your bed &
Take off

And then I wrote, "Things change—some don't change. We
change—but not really. Life goes on."

*

"Louie is going to share another poem of his with us."

"You're a poet? Oh, now it all makes sense!"

"And, Marit, you're going to translate it into Norwegian, yes?"

"Oh no!"

Gregory nudges her. "You *have* to do it."

"And since we don't know Norwegian you can make it up, you can translate it anyway you want."

"I need a pause. I cannot focus."

"Maybe it's the noise."

"Maybe I had too much to drink last night."

"It'd be so nice."

"You don't have to do anything original. Just repeat whatever you hear in Norwegian. We'll listen to you and write new versions. Another thing we could do it translate all the stupid sounds around us."

"The noise is *really* terrible."

"Terrible!"

"It reminds me of the dentist!"

"Don't they take a lunch break or something? Maybe we should go over and suggest to them that it's a good time to have a sandwich and a coffee."

"Maybe we could *bring* them a sandwich and a coffee."

"See, the great thing about this is that we're all going to mishear the poem."

"It's New York City."

"So we'll each write down what we hear when she reads."

"Marit, your participation is essential for this to work."

"I will turn on my superbrain in a moment."

"Louie, we're ready, do you want to share your poem with us?"

"Now I can't find it. Wait. I found it. It's a short one, a political one."

"Good. We need political poems."

> Poetry meets reality.
> We told the agents from ICE
> as we surrounded them
> that if they wanted to deport
> the immigrants
> they would have to take us too
> and they did.

Marit turns it into:

> *Poesi møter realitet*
> *Agentat ble informet te IS*
> *som vi omgive de*
> *de ville deportere immigranten*
> *de måtte ta oss også*
> *og de gjorde de*

Gregory introduces his version: "This is a stark poem that is going to rouse the masses."

> You see much real treats
> Again play it to these trees
> Some see a unity
> These willing impressive immigrants
> Three much of tar-autos
> Oh the horrordays!

"Nice. Does it have a title? Louie, does yours have a title?"

"Poem slash rant."

"What would that be in Norwegian?"

"*Poesi slash rant.*"

"I don't have a title yet. How about 'Stopping by the Trees on a Loud Afternoon.'"

"Good one. Who wants to go next? Here's mine, titled 'Slasher Rant.'"

Poèsie and such an intercept
I can't play informant for ICE
Zombie, you're frozen, eh?
TV granting the migrante
No deed, muck and tar, oh so…
Oh dear, you're not dead

"I like it. I like it," says Lew. María goes next.

What is reality?
What is real?
Against what are we fighting?
Some say we're not ready.
Where are the immigrants?
We have all multiplied.
How awesome we are all united.

Their daughter Lina at some point had showed up with a very quiet Chihuahua. She's also participating.

Who sees the reality
Against the play of the país
Son, the humility
Débil de inmigrante
The multitude of osos
Oh the EEUU de ti

"I love 'the multitude of osos.'"

*

"Does anybody speak a language other than Spanish or Norwegian?"

"German. I'll read you something. How about the opening lines of a Rilke poem."

> *Stiller Freund der vielen Fernen, fühle,*
> *wie dein Atem noch den Raum vermehrt.*

"It's a great poem. 'Silent friend of many distances…'"

"There's a great stanza that will help all of us in these difficult times."

> *Und wenn dich das Irdische vergass,*
> *zu der stille Erde sag: Ich, rinne.*
> *Zu dem raschen wasser sprich: Ich bin.*

"And when the earthly has forgotten you, to the silent earth say: I'm flowing. To the rushing water say: I am."

"It's an assertion of self."

"It's Rilke at the highest level. There's another helpful one. 'Is drinking bitter to you? Become wine.'"

"You can't go wrong with Rilke."

Marit reads her version:

> *Stillhetens venn med stjernenes tillatelse*
> *Some faller ut ut i mørkets pust*
> *Sort som i det store verdensrommet*
> *mørket fremtid*

"That's really beautiful. What does it say in Norwegian?"

"I don't know if it makes any kind of sense. Actually, it talks about space, and about falling, and about darkness."

"Want to give a rough translation?"

> The friend of silence with the stars' permission
> Some fall into the darkness
> Black as in the big space
> Dark future

"It's so noisy here."

"You know, John Cage said you should welcome distraction because it can only teach you to focus."

"That's a good point."

"Oh, hi!"

"Hey. Loud, eh?"

"This is Stephen, everyone. We are here because of him."

"Awesome."

"I've seen him before."

"Join us! We're translating Rilke."

"Okay, so I'll read it slowly. Do either of you speak German?"

"No."

"That's good."

> *Stiller Freund der vielen Fernen, fühle,*
> *wie dein Atem noch den Raum vermehrt.*

"Oops, we have another participant. Hey, Clint! You might have to do it again. Come sit with us."

"No problem. I can read this poem till the cows come home."

"It's a good moment to jump in."

"I'm on my lunch break. I can't stay too long."

"Write what you hear."

> *Stiller Freund der vielen Fernen, fühle,*
> *wie dein Atem noch den Raum vermehrt.*

*

Still friends of the feeling fair
we dine at ten
knock ten vows,
Fair Mart.
Children, Freud's friend
from the file fear not
Oo la la
Die for lack of breath
Night surrounds
Fear mere (existence).

They are feeling
it's unfair.
They are attempting
To get grounded and
Wait for the miracle.

Still our friends de fieles fueren
Full of divine breath
Knock them around, fear morte!

Still a friend or field
        Thru, like a flight, video and time
                not a realm
                        fear, like near.

Still a friend we dare to be fair
Filling time and as the end
Knocking on doors

Still closed

Still a friend, dear feeling, fear none
Fool, ah!
Divine attempt
Knock them down, fear not

Silent friend of the many distances,
how your breath still enlarges space.

*

Clint leaves. Lew, Lina and María get on their way too. The
jackhammers quiet down. Now we hear birds and children at the
playground nearby.

A man with a stroller is interested in what we're doing. "Well, I've
gotta cruise around with him. He gets kind of restless, you know?
So I don't think I can sit in one spot. We might hit the playground.
Maybe we'll catch some of it later. Thanks, guys!"

"Hey, we translate baby talk too!"

*

Rebekah stops by. Her prompt is to find a person who can tell her
about their favorite words in a language that's not English.

A Chinese woman is collecting recyclables from the trash bins in
the fountain area. She waves us away.

We speak to a young woman with a roller suitcase who's on her way back home to Chicago. Her favorite words in Urdu are میری جان (*meri jaan*) and بیٹا (*beta*) and بیٹی (*beti*), the words for *son* and *daughter*. *Honey dear*, her mother would say to them when they were growing up.

*

Marit, Stephen, Gregory, Christina and I write brief poems in invented languages whose transliteration has yet to be decided upon, and thus, at the moment, remain confined to recordings of their single instance of oral delivery. It's as if each of us are possessed by spirits from distant times and places.

"It sounds like sound art or something crazy."

"That's the beauty of it."

"I think it's much more meaningful than that. It's a profound writing."

*

Before leaving Gregory writes a poem in a language that is not in his mother tongue.

> *Ich fahre und fliege und ab und en*
> *laufe und dann Komme zurück.*
> *Odernichts. Ich bin nicht sicher.*
> *Alles ist anders. Die Vogel sind*

Freunde, andere Tiere auch. Die
Ferne sind Freundlich, Ich liebe die
Welt. Und ziemlich viele Leute.
Die Berge sind Freunde. Ich bin
ein Freund von meinen Freunden.

I travel and fly and every now and then
walk and come and then return
or not. I am not certain.
Everything is different. The birds are
friends, other animals are also. The
distances are friendly, I love the
world. And quite a number of people.
The mountains are friends. I'm a
friend of my friends.

"You know where this comes from? When Mandelstam was
dragged before Stalin's troops, he was like, 'What do you want of me?
I am the colleague of Anna Akhmatova. I am a friend of my friends.'
And he knows that as soon as he says this he's going to be killed."

"Wow. Could you have written this poem in English?"

"Probably not. It has a different rhythm in German. In English it
would sound hokey."

"We heard it first in German and then in the English. We were let
in by the German. We dropped our guards and slipped in. Or, better,
the poem slipped into our ears."

*

Again the day's session ends with our efforts to resuscitate defunct words.

intérlope (n.)
>   1. A four-legged mammal resulting from the cross of an interpreter and an antelope.
>   2. One who mediates between two parties.
>   3. To go inside the wrong way (the act of).

nipos (conj.)
>   1. *ni por favor / ni pero*
>   Neither *please* nor *but*, but *maybe*.

nipos (n.)
>   1. Japanese soybean snacks for those allergic to peanuts.
>   2. Nephews.

ofideido (adj.)
>   1. atfeedaywent
>   when the day is over,
>   and it felt like it
>   cost a lot, with nothing (or not enough) gained
>   (where is god here?)

ofideido (n.)
>   1. One who cannot commit to a choice, an indecisive person.
>   2. A small round plastic case mounted on a ring to transport microscopic objects on your finger.

"If a message circulating on social networking sites like Twitter and Facebook is to be believed, **Bengali** has been voted the sweetest language in the world. Conducted by Unesco, the vote ranks **Spanish** and **Dutch** as the second and third sweetest tongues respectively." Apr 22, 2010

Sweetest language tag for Bengali? - Times of India
indiatimes.com › timesofindia › india › a...

About this result   Feedback

Why is Bengali called one of the sweetest languages in the world? Why does it ...
Quora · Why-is-Bengali-called-one-of-th...

So, it will be ignorant of me to call Bengali as the 'sweetest language in the world' in spite of the that Bengali is my mother language. Howev definitely point out several reasons why Ber considered a sweet language both by native speakers and many non-native speakers and even non-speakers.

I notice a man reading the "Poetry will be made by all" poster. He's on his lunch break and works at Charles Schwab. Michael is his name. He's Chinese and says he's a bad poet.

"Doesn't matter to me. Let me ask you something: Is there an idiomatic expression equivalent to 'The writing on the wall' in Chinese?'" He stares at me blankly. I rephrase the question.

"Well, at around 4 am there's the darkness before the bright. And before the storm, it gets so quiet. It's a warning. In China idioms are based on what some famous person said once. In Asia too, before war starts, both sides are very very quiet, before they charge each other."

"So it's like the quiet before the storm then."

I ask Ramis, an intern from Bangladesh, if there's an idiom for "The writing on the wall" in Bangla.

"I don't know," she says. "Let me brainstorm."

"What does that mean?"

Ramis beats me to explaining the phrase to Michael: "It's like thinking a lot, in your mind. There's wind and maybe some rain, and you think so much your brain acts like a storm."

*

Ramis tells me about her language. I mean, languages. "Wait, how many do you speak?"

"Urdu, Hindi, Bangla, and English."

"I learned some Urdu words the day before: *meri jaan*."

Jaan is also a word in Bangla and Hindi (जान), and it means *heart* and *life*. She also tells me that hers is the only country in the world in which people have sacrificed their lives to save their language.

"Pakistan and Bangladesh were once one country. We were known as East Pakistan and Pakistan was known as West Pakistan. Things were kind of unfair back then, like, there were a lot of political leaders forcing us to not speak Bangla and to use Urdu as the primary language instead. People in the east refused to do so. 'No, you can't separate our mother tongues from us, we'd rather give up our lives. Our language is our heritage.' So students from University of Dhaka rallied in the street to protest and, while they were doing so, Pakistani soldiers tried to stop them. They kept protesting, so five students were shot dead."

"What year is this?"

"1952. 21st February. That date is known as the International Mother Tongue day. We have a national monument and every year, on 21st February, people go there in the early morning and give flowers to the sacrificed souls."

She Googles pictures of the Shaheed Minar. "The tall structure in the middle is the mother, and the red circle is her heart. It shows grief. And to her sides are her children: two sons and two daughters. Bangla was voted the sweetest language in the world by UNESCO. It's simple and sweet-sounding."

*

Michael's back. He's checked the Chinese at the office and has brought me a printout of the equivalent for "the writing on the wall" in Chinese characters.

"Google is not very good. This is the right Chinese for 'the writing on the wall.' The amazing thing is that in my company nobody knows this saying."

"That's what's great about sayings. You ask people what they mean or where they come from and often people don't know."

"Right. 'You see the light at the end of the tunnel.' That's really good. Everybody knows what that means." He says goodbye and returns to his office.

*

I go use the restroom for the park's staff under the Shake Shack and when I get back my friend Ying is there. I show her Michael's printout, and she tells Ramis and I what each character means.

"Super imminent sign for a super bad event about to happen. These characters say urgent eyelashes bad/violent omen. Something's so urgent it's right in front of your eyelashes."

緊急的睫毛壞兆頭暴力預兆

For "the quiet before the storm" she gives us: "Mountain rain about to come, wind fills the mansion, or prostitution house or tower."

"All right, this is what we're doing. You broke down the Chinese characters in the idioms, but I'd like us to rearrange the items to say different things. That's what I'd like us to play with."

"So we're going to use these words to form sentences?"

"Yeah, string them in any way you want and add anything you'd like. Let's each of us do it first into our own languages and then translate them into English. For example, something like: Her eyelashes fell off as she was rushing to the mountain."

"In Bangla?"

"Yes, and then you'll translate that into English. Just have fun with it."

"Oh, also this character can also mean desire: 欲. Use that if you want."

*

We're approached by a woman called Núria, from Mallorca. I thought I heard she's shooting a video about women's sexuality for a TV show in Barcelona. She asks Ramis if she's willing to answer a few questions on camera, and Ramis eagerly agrees.

"Wait, what exactly did she ask you?"

"'What's the most sensitive part of a vagina? I forgot the name.' And I'm like, 'Clitoris.' And she goes, 'Oh yeah, I remember from biology classes but it was a long time ago...' Then she asked me if I ever received oral..."

"That was her question?"

"Yeah!"

"From where?" Ying hadn't noticed they were filming. "It's a TV show?"

"It's for a YouTube channel called Scary Mommy, it's comedy. Today the topic was 'Madge the Vag.' And then she asked me if I'd receive it and I said I wouldn't because from my classes I know it's not hygienic. Health comes first."

Ying laughs.

"'What would you do if someone went up there?' And I'm like, 'Hit him in the face. Karate chops. Done.'"

"What's the word for clitoris in Bangla?"

"I don't know."

"I don't know the word in Chinese either."

"You don't? Come on!"

"Maybe it's G diǎn, g-點. G-point. But I don't know if it's the same thing as the clitoris."

"G-spot. That's the spot where a girl receives the highest form of pleasure."

"But it's not necessary the clitoris. The clitoris is the protuberance, the organ."

"I even heard that guys also have a G-spot."

"They do? Where?"

"It has to be the tip of their penis."

"Maybe it's in their balls, I don't know."

"How do you say balls in Bangla and in Chinese?"

"In Chinese it's eggs: 蛋蛋 *dàn dàn*. You say it twice. One is a smaller egg and the other one is slightly bigger."

*

We set out to write. "One thing to keep in mind when you translate is that this is not about smoothing things out, but about retaining the weirdness of going from one language to the other."

"This is so hard! It's embarrassing!"

"Don't think about it in terms of whether it's good or bad poetry, but of could you have produced this if you hadn't refracted the lines from one language to another?"

"Yeah. I'm a little confused myself."

"You can always change it if you don't like it. No one's judging."

Ying goes first.

> rain showers   mountain brow
> shy peak frightens its bra
> who wants to kill
> wind blows
> and it breaks skin

Núria shows up. "I'm ready. I have five minutes." Ramis had dutifully asked her to come by our table when she was done interviewing so she could participate in our project in return. "How do you say 'share' in Spanish?"

"*Compartir.*"

"*Vamos a compartir.*"

> On the walls of the mountain are
> written some urgent words,
> words of storm,
> words will form stories.
>
> *La casa se llena de viento y lluvia*
> *cuando la tormenta silente del deseo se precipita.*
> *Sabemos que se avecina algo terrible,*
> *está escrito en la pared.*
> *No es graffiti. Mis pestañas urgentes*
> *lo tienen en las narices.* It's not graffiti
> what is written on the wall.

My urgent eyelashes have it right on their noses.
The storm will become our neighbor.

La pluja urgent, omple les meves
pestanyes senyalant un oscur devenir.
The urgent rain fills my eyelashses
predicting a bad omen.

*

Ying and I look at Ramis's original lines in Bangla in order to pro-
duce versions based on the visual shapes we see embedded in the script.

bean sprout dozen sweet sixteen
senior arrow / spoon grape lamp cherry on top
gate music note hot wire / dog breast-feeding
tangled triangle max / infant unborn downward
dog fetus pose

I see numbers, a dime a dozen, but it isn't actually a dime.
It's more like 54. Those were the days, of Studio 54.
The next word is like dancing, like doing a conga line,
and ending up on the floor, bum up.
How alive these words seem. If that is an H it is a wide
one for all of us to take silent shelter in.
"From A to B is what I hear," is what I overhear, though
again, it doesn't apply to tagging, which is what I
keep seeing.
Signage with upside-down i's and, periods facing down,
since we're engaged in girl talk. Compressed, I spotted
the word *Stockholm*.

Stephen comes by again later that day with Libby, his mom. They recombine the definitions that Ying had given us in poems of their own.

HOW QUIET IS THIS PROSTITUTION HOUSE

> how quiet are omens
> in towers, through equals
> violet renderings
>> no light
>> so blinking (highways)
> marked with rain
> eyelashes filled

> Behind the eyelashes
> perhaps bad omen, urgent
> quiet storm.
> Tower of omen, equals
> before the slow, urgent
> like mountain rain

PLEASED SO PLEASED VERY VERY PLEASED

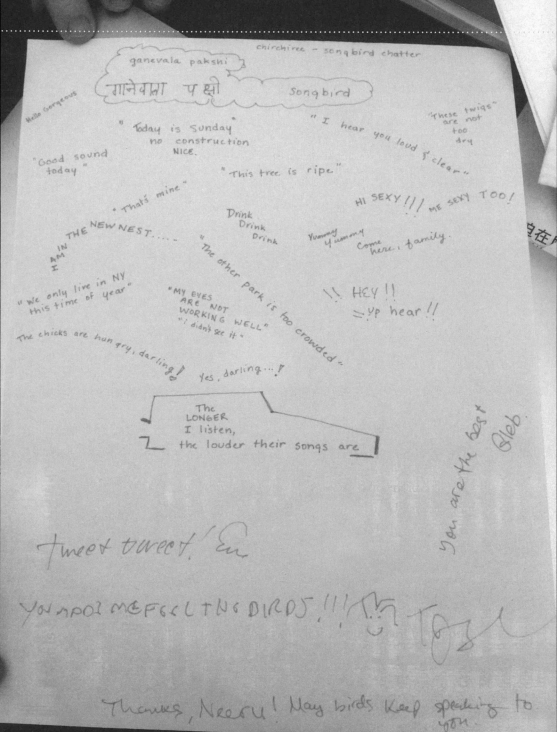

Train delays again. I get to the park and see people sitting around the table I'll occupy today. I rush toward them to find out that no, they're not here for poetry. It's a group of German students. I ask what the phrase *"Alle werden Dichter sein"* in the poster means.

"Everyone will be poet. They're not doing it right now, but everyone will do it in the future."

"I asked my friend Sabine to translate the phrase, and she told me that you can't *make* poetry in German. You have to... What is the word?"

"*Machen*... You have to *be* a poet."

"So you don't *write* poetry, you *are* a poet?"

"Yeah. That's more common."

"So if you write one poem one day and never write a poem again, does that make you a poet?"

"No, in German, no."

"So you're just a poet while you're writing a poem?"

"Yeah. You are a poet when you write *ballades*."

"There is a subject: *Dichtung*. It means poetry, but nobody uses it."

"Why?"

"Because it has another meaning, but it's very different. When you're in the bathroom..."

"Oh no! *Nein nein.*"

"It's a double-meaning. In the shower there's a hole and that's a *Dichtung.*"

"A drain?"

"No, the thing in the hole, so the water doesn't go."

"What are wheels made of? It's a rubber thing."

"A stopper!"

"Oh, a stopper. That's *Dichtung*?"

"I think there is an explanation. The adjective *Dicht* means *dense* or *tight*. *Dichtung* derives from *dicht.*"

"Fascinating. See, you already contributed to the poem. Thanks so much!"

*

Kate chooses to "write in a language that is not the mother tongue."

Andy and Zazie show up. "Kate is writing in French. When she's done, we're going to play a game. We're going to listen very closely to her as she reads, and we will write down what we hear. Maybe we'll hear words in English."

"This is good. Zazie, you can't write words, can you?"

"She can draw pictures."

"Zazie, you just listen and tell your dad what you hear."

"I think I have a better idea: I'll just draw a picture of what I hear."

"You got it. Strange weather today."

"Yesterday's weather was strange too."

"It's one of those days when you look at the temperature and it says 72 degrees but it's freezing outside! I don't understand."

"Or like when it says 68 degrees and you go out and it's super hot. It's the humidity."

"Yeah. Between 68 and 73 degrees, that's the mystery zone."

*

Kate begins reading.

> *Zazie ne comprend pas français, plutôt espagnol est sa langue.*

"That's you, Zazie."

> *avec Monica mon ami, professional poète*

"I think *poète* means poetry."

"Yep, I wrote that down, Zaz."

"Great. I figured out what it means!"

J'admet que j'ai tendance à remarquer ce qui est idiosyncrasique chez les gens. Par exemple, lorsque Monica parle, sa bouche et ses lèvres favorisent un côté, mais ses dents sont toujours au milieu. Ça lui va bien. Ça fait l'aire d'une non-conformiste, comme elle est, évidemment!

A passerby waves at me. "Hi! Are you the artist?"

"Yes. I mean, no. I'm not the artist, I'm the poet."

Quoi de neuf avec moi…? Chez, ma famille… mon mari es maintenant dessous le ciel—le ciel de coton! Il reviens d'Inde ou il séjournait. In English: « India ». L'heure, pour lui dans son propre expérience est bien un demi jour à l'envers de la nôtre. C'est up-side down. La bonne nouvelle c'est qu'il a mangé de bons cornichons a Bangalore.
Içi dans le parc se trouve le Flat Iron bâtiment trianglul-aire-(air!) Elle est notre propre forteresse.
Ma rêve c'est de louer un petit bureau là-haut, où je pourrais être dans les nuages comme l'avion qui transport mon mari.

J'ECOUTE ET C'EST DOUX; LES BRUIT LES NOISES DES CLOUDES.

"What've you got, man?"

Andy jumps right in. "I'll just read what I have."

ZAZIE DOESN'T UNDERSTAND FRENCH

Set Spanish, Pluto park comfort
I am flirting with Monica
My professional poet friend

I hummus easy idiosyncratic movement today
For example, Monica precisely speaking
Encounter a bush, nonconformist me
Oh sausage of me, how nine, my house,
New sacred revenues in New York
But no! With you, rabbit
sky of crouton
Assman day in India
The proper dance experience
Conversation with other
Our house customary English cuisine prison
Good eating little mirror
Mashed pickles
It's odor I hear, I breathe the noises.

"Yesssss. Amazing!"

"Assman day in India! Are you a poet by nature?"

"No. Zazie helped me with rabbit; she heard *conejo* which *en español* means rabbit."

This one is Zazie's interpretation:

"Can you explain the drawing to us? What's happening?"

"That's what she's saying and that's me hearing it."

"Is the sound coming out of the monkey's ear?"

"It's not a monkey! It's me!"

"Here's mine."

ZAZIE

Say *futból*, *español*, parlay and comprehend.
Pro fay, the movement, idiosyncratic,
the john, per not conform.
History, paranormal precision.
And Sue had dental work but hadn't conformed
to the dentist.
Oh, so Joe did not sue.
Joe is just married and moved
to New York with El Otro,
a seal who cut dough.
The assman is going to India.
On Ingres, they dance. Puppets experience
and drink Evian
while they converse about Notre-Dame.
I suppose *entre nous*, it's customary.
Too dire English, too Trump's ire,
cuisine, the bon mot
pataphysical and queer.
But *le cornichon*
I gnashed.

Say, Ralph, why am I alone?
I listen and I do the brutish noises of clouds.

"Woohoo! Nothing wrong with that one!"

"This is a good game."

"I like it because I'm just free writing. And if I'm going to write a poem it has to be things that I notice. For instance, I noticed that you speak precisely, and often from one side of your mouth, and that your teeth are like lace. But nonconformist lace."

"That's so true! No one's ever noticed that."

"Ha!"

I am as struck by the truth of Kate's observation of my asymmetrical mouth movements as Andy is by the mention of nonconformist lace.

Kate leaves.

*

Melinda shows up, and then Janice. Bruce introduces her to all.

"Zazie, how about you go find someone who speaks another language besides English?" She and Melinda go off to the playground together.

"So when you're introduced, I'm always confused, Andrew or Andy?"

"I like to see what people pick."

195

"I found two people but they didn't want to come!" Zazie and Melinda go off to the playground again.

"What do you prefer being called?"

"The one that I don't like is Mr. Andy. Mr. Andy sounds like a real creep to me."

"Mr. Andy sounds close to Andy Griffiths's Mayberry."

*

"Hey! We found someone!"

"It worked!"

"Fantastic! Good job, guys!"

"Welcome! What language do you speak?"

"Punjabi."

"Great. Thanks for joining!" Maya, Rashmi's daughter, starts playing with Zazie.

"It's easy! It's family friendly!"

"Do you have a favorite poem in Punjabi?"

"Oh gosh, no. Hindi maybe, but not Punjabi. Maybe my dad does."

"Can you translate 'Poetry will be made by all' into Punjabi?"

"Dad, how do you say *poetry* in Punjabi?"

"*Shayari.*"

"*Shayari*, yes! It's hard, because it says 'will be made.'"

"Could be made, should be made..."

"Each translation is slightly different."

"Daddy, how do you say 'Poetry will be made by all'?"

"I don't know."

"He's the one born in India! My mind's all over the place."

*

"Everybody, I have an idea. This is what we'll do: translate bird-song, clouds, or ambient noise. You have ten minutes to walk around and write down what you hear. Listening to birds might be best, because it's nice and quiet in the park today."

Even though it's Saturday afternoon, the park is almost empty. It's windy and chilly. The first cold day of the season. Birds aren't as active as I'd like them to be right now.

"So you actually want me to write, 'The birds go tweet, tweet' type of thing?"

"Write what you're hearing."

"Maybe you hear them speak to you, or to each other. Whatever you feel like."

Greg is back today. His back hurts because he was sitting and chanting with the Hare Krishnas and is carrying a backpack full of books.

"The same happens to me when I'm schlepping books all day long."

They all come back. "Rashmi, do you want to start?"

Aa-o aa-o aa-o	(Come, come, come!)
Menu klao menu klao menu klao	(Feed me, feed me, feed me!)
Uo-row Uo-row	(Fly, fly!)
Nacho, nacho, gaho, gaho	(Dance, dance, sing, sing,
Merai naal aa-o	come with me!")
Menu t-and lagdhee hai ... menu vee	(I'm feeling cold ... me too!)
Mera peechai naa aa-o	(Don't run after me!)

"Birds really sing in Punjabi."

"Exactly! They do!" All agree.

Janice reads what she heard.

>sweet sweet sweet
>clip
>luck luck
>sappy snappy snappy
>twist twist
>sweet sweet

"Ha, sweet!"

"So playing with that, I was trying to just transcribe everything, the different sounds that were going by, both words and sound."

>Shyly waaaa haaaa like
>ooops frikkkkk anyway this is all
>sssssshhhhhhh
>we were there and we went out
>what a weird place to go
>ah ahh jingling metal ahgg
>ah yeah I do not beeeep
>clack clack wow that's crazy
>hahaha (fast) you, can I talk to you?

"Bruce! He's so good at this kind of thing."

A loud helicopter goes by.

"Mine is different," says Andy. "I tried to get close to people who weren't speaking English, and then tried to make what they said into English. Then a few sounds roll in."

So that this is over
Five more minutes this weekend
Constructing yawns
folding chairs collapsing
Old McDonald's had a honk
up to right now I forget
How are we doing on zebra lines?
Someone, turn on the tap
Too cold for ice cream
Not for me
Why don't you get cold
It's fine, it's okay, it's like
All of my friends are there
The growl of no

*

"Let's see. I really didn't get too many birds sounds in this one. I described the sound more than got the sound itself,'" said Greg before he read his poem with pauses in between the lines, since he couldn't read his handwriting.

Thin reedy chirp of lonely bird, his chirp all alone as
birch leaf by birch leaf twirl and float to ground.
Corner of Broadway and 26th, yellow cabs slip by grey
squirrels and pigeons who will not sing. A wedding
party snaps pics, maids in taupe silk and white roses.

Cross 25th St. loop and black heels click past.
Small dog barks before I hear the reedy *cherou cherou*
of tiny birds I never waited long in Gotham to kiss my ears.
Gnarled old crabapple twists as if in suffocation

for songs, but not a single wing lands on bough.
Dog parks walks but scare the little birds so we move
past with a pair of pugs to playground.
Saturday black beret blossomed in front of
Chihuahua in a tiny grey hoodie. Baby chases

pigeons past Japanese red maple. Still no song
to be heard by Flat Iron families out of condo boxes
for the day. High above a whippoorwill
sounds. Where have all the birdsongs gone?

Why, off to Central Park, where solitude is long &
freedom voices of birdsong sing.

"That's *really* nice."

"I was straining there at the end."

"Mine is short, since I was holding the fort."

We don't tweet!
So we've chosen, on this windy day, to remain
                    inaudible.

Right?
Totally, yes.
¿Y? ¿Y?   And?
Weird.
¡Ahí viene la ardilla!
What? What? A squirrel?
Sweet, not tweet?
This is skewed.

Everyone laughs. "Definitely, though, birds sing in Punjabi."

*

Alan, Karla, Sophie, and Peter come by.

"Okay, let me turn on the recorder now."

"All creativity will now vanish from the tent," Alan jokes.

Sophie's been learning Latin at school by focusing on the vocab in the different chapters of a book. She says she knows random verbs and names and stuff. She writes a couple of sentences in Latin and Alan and Karla translate them by sound.

> *Puella nomine Karla sedet sub arbore et scribit.*
> *Puer nomine Alan ascendit arbore.*
> *Sedio in magnus hortus.*

"So homophonic translations just mean you follow the sounds?"

"It's most fun when you try to translate those sounds into English words, as opposed to just transcribe the sounds. I'm still trying to learn that myself."

"So 'pulled no my car…'"

"Don't say it yet, just write it all down!"

"I'm just trying to get this party started!"

Pulled no my car lost sea bet our bore it scribbled.
Pure nominee a land's end it are board.
Ceiling may grab us horrible.

"So what does the Latin actually say?"

A girl named Karla sat under the tree and wrote.
A boy named Alan climbed the tree.
I sit in the big garden.

*

"Let's play dictionary and resuscitate some words again." It's almost
five and Peter can't stay. "You guys pick the words."

jifero (n.)

    1. A heavy star.

    2. New calf.

    3. Sun.

    4. Spanish pronunciation of Heathrow Airport.

    5. Pile of bricks.

    6. A feral giraffe from the Bolivian plains.

kora (n.)

    1. Small shells at the shoreline.

    2. Song.

    3. Coral.

    4. Coral without a partner.

    5. Shoal of bluefish.

    6. A salad bar for people to grab something to hold them over
while in Purgatory.

ñanga (n.)
1. The smooth inside of cheeks.
2. Goat.
3. Mango.
4. Grandmother version of manga.
5. A negation of *ga*. *Ga*: verb to see.
6. A panda from Latin America.

*

"Hey, are you the binocular people?"

"The binocular people? No."

He grunts, "What's going on?"

"Making up words!"

"I don't have a couple hundred thousand grand. I'm short of twenty million. I'm poor, you know."

He's making noises that compete with the helicopter above.

"That's New York too, you know. Random encounters."

Sophie's cold, so Alan, Karla, and her get on their way.

*

A man named Vijay walks by, from Mumbai. I ask him to tell me what the word for *border* is in his language. He knows more than one language. The word is *sīmā*, सीमा, which is Marathi for *edge*, *bank*, and *margin.* I'm asking because I'm interested in the words other languages have for *border*, and because in Spanish there is one word used for the border between abstractions such as national territories—*frontera*—and another for the border of tangible things: *borde.*

"We say music is beyond borders, for instance. In Marathi it would be: संगीत सीमाबाहेर आहे (*saṅgīta sīmābāhēra āhē*)."

"Do you write poetry?"

"I write poetry in Marathi. I wrote a poem a few days ago, about activities going on in the city."

"Earlier today someone who speaks Punjabi helped us translate birdsong into Punjabi. It sounds like birds sing in Punjabi. Would you do that in Marathi?"

"Oh, no! Animal noises are different. Crows go *cao cao* and sparrows *chick chick chick*... so many things like that. Cows go *hmm hmm.*"

"I'm always doing that. I must be a cow, definitely *not* a sacred one."

"All animals are sacred because everybody has heart, everybody has soul. The trees have soul, आत्मा, *Ātmā.*"

"The script is beautiful."

"*Devanagari*: देवनागरी." He pronounces all the vowels and consonants very fast, to comical effect.

"That just sounded like a sound poem. Do you know sound poetry?"

"Yes. In *My Fair Lady*, Prof. Higgins uses sound poetry to impress Audrey Hepburn and teach her to speak good English: 'The rain in Spain falls mainly on the plain.'"

"Can I make a move?"

"Pardon me?"

"Can I go now?"

"Yes! Of course! I'm so sorry to keep you. Nice to talk with you."

"Not at all! I enjoyed it very much too. It's just my friend…"

*

"Maybe we should just listen to some poetry now. I brought my portable speaker."

"What's that sound? Birdsong?"

"It's just the laptop's sounds."

"I'm hearing phantom birdsong everywhere."

"We'll hear some Gertrude Stein now. What would you like to hear? 'A Portrait of T.S. Eliot,' an excerpt from *The Making of Americans*, or 'If I Told Him, A Completed Portrait of Picasso'?"

"Maybe the Picasso?"

"Yeah, the Picasso."

… Was there was there was there what was there was there what was there was there there was there.

Whether and in there.
As even say so.
One.
I land.
Two.
I land.
Three.
The land.
Three
The land.
Three.
The land.
Two
I land.
Two
I land.
One
I land.
Two
I land.
As a so.
The cannot.
A note.
They cannot
A float.
They cannot.
They dote.
They cannot.

They as denote.
Miracles play.
Play fairly.
Play fairly well.
A well.
As well.
As or as presently.
...

PROMPTS

+ "One should write in a language that is not the mother tongue."
(Vicente Huidobro, *Altazor*, tr. by Eliot Weinberger)

+ Find someone from another country and ask him or her to tell you their favorite word in their own language.

+ Find false friends.

+ Resuscitate words.

+ Invent a language.

+ Translate ambient noise.

+ Translate bird song.

+ Pick an idiomatic expression and ask someone who speaks a different language for an equivalent in that language. Examples: "the writing's on the wall"; "drown your sorrows"; "sweep under the rug."

+ How do you say "border" in your language? Find equivalents.

+ What is to translate? Translate translate.

+ Write in one language as if it were another.

+ Do a homophonic or homographic translation.

+ Write a poem using an untranslatable word.

ACKNOWLEDGMENTS

Versions of the poems in this book have appeared in the following
publications:

The Animated Reader, edited by Brian Droitcour (New Museum),
*Big Big Wednesday, The Brooklyn Rail, Critical Quarterly, Das Magazin,
Folder, The Literary Review, Murmur: An Anthology, The Paris Review,
Poem-A-Day, Postscript: Writing After Conceptual Art* edited by Andrea
Andersson (Toronto, 2018), *Seung-Taek Lee* (Lévy Gorvy, 2017),
Stonecutter

I am thankful for the support of their respective editors, and especially
Andrea Andersson, Anselm Berrigan, Phong Bui, Rory Cook, Brian
Droitcour, Sylvia Gorelick, Ruth Ellen Kocher, Ben Lerner, Valeria
Luiselli, Aditi Machado, Minna Proctor, and Molly Schaeffer. I owe
"137 Northeast Regional" to an invitation from Julie Carr to write
an epistolary piece for the "Borrowed Confessions" program at Poets
House in 2017.

A series of prints from the *Equivalencias* series was included in the
exhibition *Postscript: Writing After Conceptual Art* curated by Nora
Burnett Abrams and Andrea Andersson. It traveled to the following
museums: Museum of Contemporary Art Denver; The Power Plant
Contemporary Art Gallery, Toronto; and Eli & Edythe Broad Art
Museum, Michigan State University in 2014.

I am enormously grateful to Polina Kovaleva at the Eurasia division of
PEN America, Maria Stepanova, Colta.ru, and Matvei Yankelevich
for inviting to Moscow in the spring of 2018 to collaborate with
Georgii Martirosian, Sergey Sdobnov, Lena Vaneyan, and Ekaterina
Zakharkiv on translations of my poems into Russian. To all: Спасибо
вам от всего сердца!

Replay was made possible thanks to an invitation from Poets House
to participate in Josiah McElheny's *Prismatic Park* collaborative

public art project. My residency at Madison Square Park took place from Sept. 27–Oct. 1, 2017. All my gratitude goes to Stephen Motika for inviting me to participate and to Josiah McElheny for his art and generosity in providing an incomparable forum for my experiment in collaborative writing. My collaborators were exceptionally enthusiastic and the work is dedicated to them, in gratitude for their openness of heart. They are (in order of appearance): Lila Zemborain, Farnoosh Fathi, Marina Blitshteyn, Ying Liu, Steven Hyland, Alina (from Ukraine), LJ Sconzo, Fran and her friend Barbara O. Byrne, Greg Duva, Josiah McElheny, Liz Madans, Stephen Motika, Gregory Volk, Marit Følstad, Clinton Krute, Christina Lynch, Rebekah Smith, Lew Grupper, María Grupper, Lina Ortiz Grupper, Michael from Charles Schwab, Ramis Rawnak, Libby Motika, Stephen Motika, Núria (from Barcelona), Kate Shepherd, Andrew Lampert, Zazie Lampert, Melinda Shopsin, Bruce Pearson, Janice Guy, Rashmi Gill, Alan Gilbert, Karla Kelsey, Sophie Prevallet, Vijay (from Mumbai). My thanks go to all the anonymous participants as well.

Laura Hoptman's expert suggestions led me to the book's title. I am much obliged.

I am grateful to Brown University's Literary Arts Department for having me as visiting professor from 2016-19. My work with faculty and students as Bonderman Professor of the Practice was indispensable.

A Lucas Arts Residency at the Montalvo Arts Center made invaluable resources available to me in the summers of 2017 and 2018. I am grateful for the center's support. Special thanks to Lori Wood. Annette Leddy, gracias siempre.

To Steel Stillman and Jane Ayers, all my thanks for that room in Peanut Cottage on Squirrel Island where I was able to reconnect with Don Quixote.

All my thanks to go to Rochelle Feinstein. Without her friendship and generosity I doubt this book would have been possible.

Thank you to my students and colleagues at Brooklyn College; I'm thrilled to be among you.

Carla Herrera-Prats (1973–2019) invited me to present some of this work at SOMA Summer in Mexico City in 2017. Her courage and dedication will remain an inspiration.

Thanks to the Nightboat crew for going above and beyond: Stephen Motika, Lindsey Boldt, Andrea Abi-Karam, Caelan Nardone, and Brian Hochberger. Les estaré siempre agradecida for their care and vision in making this book.

To Bruce, my parents, Jenny, Ernesto, and Cathy, beyond gratitude, as ever.

MÓNICA DE LA TORRE is the author of *The Happy End/All Welcome*, published by Ugly Duckling Presse, which also put out her translation of *Defense of the Idol* by Chilean modernist Omar Cáceres. Other books of hers include *Public Domain* and *Talk Shows*, as well as *Acúfenos* and *Sociedad Anónima* published in Mexico City. Born and raised there, she has lived in New York City since the 1990s. She teaches poetry at Brooklyn College.

NIGHTBOAT BOOKS

Nightboat Books, a nonprofit organization, seeks to develop audiences for writers whose work resists convention and transcends boundaries. We publish books rich with poignancy, intelligence, and risk. Please visit nightboat.org to learn about our titles and how you can support our future publications.

The following individuals have supported the publication of this book. We thank them for their generosity and commitment to the mission of Nightboat Books:

Kazim Ali
Anonymous
Jean C. Ballantyne
Photios Giovanis
Amanda Greenberger
Elizabeth Motika
Benjamin Taylor
Peter Waldor
Jerrie Whitfield & Richard Motika

In addition, this book has been made possible, in part, by grants from the National Endowment for the Arts and the New York State Council on the Arts Literature Program.